ENDORSEMENTS

In this book Ryan equips you with practical tools to activate your faith and receive prophetic promises. You will discover how to bring the super into your natural.

JASON ARMSTRONG
Founder of Remnant Fire Ministries
Associate Pastor Summit Church
TN State Leader Heartland Apostolic Prayer Network

Ryan Johnson has woven together a tapestry in *How to Contend for Your Miracle* that will equip you in understanding the importance of faith, hope and trust in the Lord. From the richness of the Word of God to the first-hand personal accounts of faith in action, you will be blessed and empowered to stand firm in the prophetic promises of a faithful God over your life."

DAWN HILL
Prophetic Writer and Blogger, The Lovesick Scribe

How to Contend for Your Miracle is more than a book on faith. It is the rendering of Ryan's real gift of digging deep into the unexplored caverns of the Word. These writings incorporate so much of the Word of God that one cannot deny the authenticity. Absorbing the contents of this book, will give exponential growth to new faith, breathe life into weakened or lethargic faith, and fortify strong faith that will not be denied, as promises turn into provision! One cannot read it without gaining eyes to "see" the unseen!

BARBARA HENSLEY
Pastor, The Upper Room Church

This book is a must read. Throughout this book, Ryan lays down a pathway for seeing the prophetic realized in your life. When you marry faith with the prophetic, the results are powerful! As you read this, allow the Holy Spirit to build your faith and watch how God moves in your life!

JOSHUA GAY
Pastor, High Praise Orlando

How to
CONTEND
for Your
MIRACLE

*How Supernatural Encounters and Faith Work
Together to Bring Answered Prayers*

RYAN JOHNSON

DESTINY IMAGE® PUBLISHERS, INC.

P.O. Box 310, Shippensburg, PA 17257-0310

"Promoting Inspired Lives."

This book and all other Destiny Image and Destiny Image Fiction books are available at Christian bookstores and distributors worldwide.

Cover design by Eileen Rockwell
Interior design by Terry Clifton

For more information on foreign distributors, call 717-532-3040.

Reach us on the Internet: www.destinyimage.com.

ISBN 13 TP: 978-0-7684-5157-3
ISBN 13 eBook: 978-0-7684-5158-0
ISBN 13 HC: 978-0-7684-5160-3
ISBN 13 LP: 978-0-7684-5159-7

For Worldwide Distribution, Printed in the U.S.A.
1 2 3 4 5 6 7 8 / 24 23 22 21 20

CONTENTS

FOREWORD

A unique set of influences laid a foundation for my faith and my near-immediate introduction to prophetic ministry. My first church experience—if you can call it that—was an unexpected encounter with bold evangelists in a grim county jail consumed with the power of death. I was facing five years in prison for a crime I didn't commit and had hit proverbial rock bottom.

Amid the criminals arguing and correctional officers belting commands, the testimonies of these evangelists—former convicts and drug addicts—released the power of hope and courage for a new beginning. I listened intently as an evangelist laid out a clear path to salvation through Jesus and the promise of "all things new." The day I accepted Christ into my heart Jesus prophesied to me directly. In effect, He showed me I would be released on the 40th day of my incarceration—with complete vindication.

It never crossed my mind not to believe Jesus's personal prophecy. I only believed. Although I was facing a five-year jail sentence, this prophetic word—which was spirit and life—inspired faith in my heart to believe it. Like Abraham, I confessed those things that were not as though they were and they came to be. Yes, I faced challenges along the path to freedom, but I activated my faith with my words over and over again. I watched as the prophetic word came to pass. I was totally vindicated and released.

When I was freed from jail I landed in an African-American Pentecostal church. It was a deliverance-oriented, prophet-led Holy Ghost congregation where prophecy was part and parcel of every service. As part of my personal wilderness experience, I landed in a Word of Faith church in a small Alabama town. Steeped in this "power of words" culture, I enrolled in Rhema Bible School and studied the works of Kenneth Hagin, Sr. and others from the Word of Faith movement. When God released me from the wilderness, I stepped square into the apostolic-prophetic movement.

After this blend of teaching, my perspective is this: Yes, we prophesy according to the proportion of our faith according to Romans 12:6. We've focused a lot on this in the early days of the prophetic movement, when believers around the world were activated to prophesy by my spiritual father, Bishop Bill Hamon. But what is also true is that you receive prophecy by faith, activate prophecy by faith, and see prophecy come to pass by faith. Put another way, personal prophecies are conditional—they are conditional on your faith and the actions your faith inspires you to take.

In *How to Contend for Your Miracle,* Ryan Johnson taps into this all-important vein—a vein that too few focus on or even understand. Many believers receive prophetic words as unconditional. They hear a prophecy at the altar, call their friends, and tell them about the wonderful word of the Lord they received, then forget about it as if it will come to pass all by itself. Ryan explains that you have to supernaturally partner with heaven to see your prophetic promises come to pass—then he gives you keys to cross the prophetic finish line.

I would urge students of faith not to brush off this book because you think you know everything there is to know about faith. There is always more to learn, more revelation to unlock—and the reality that we need to be reminded of what we know because sometimes we hear the Word and don't do it and end up deceiving ourselves. Faith is the currency of the kingdom and we need to continue studying it. Ryan has tied faith to prophetic promises in a way I have never seen done. Many people tie faith to promises in the Word, but fewer have drilled into faith to walk out a prophetic word.

If you have unfulfilled prophetic words sitting in a drawer or "on the shelf," this book will help you cultivate and release the faith required to partner with God. As I always say, God won't do our part, but we can't do His part. The good news is God will do His part and our faith will empower us to take action to see our prophetic promises manifest, whether that's getting a passport, studying for a new career—or just waiting on the Lord like Abraham did.

Ryan's book shares practical stories, sound theology, and the inspiration you need to dust off the prophecies you gave up on and believe again. As you read this book, you will come into the understanding that it's never too late to believe God—and God is never late. Many times we think we're waiting on Him when He's actually waiting on us. So whether your part is to wait, war, or "only believe," you'll get the guidance you need to glorify God with the manifestation of His will for you as you read the pages of this timely book. Thanks, Ryan, for writing it!

JENNIFER LECLAIRE
Founder, Jennifer LeClaire Ministries
Best-selling author, *The Making of a Prophet*
Senior Leader, Awakening House of Prayer

PREFACE

My family and I were visiting with our extended families after the holidays because we lived in another state. The first Sunday of January we attended my parents' home church. I vividly remember sitting in the very back of the church with my dad while my mother was on the praise and worship team. My parents' church was very familiar to my wife and children; I had been a student pastor there for a number of years, while serving several different ministries. It was a ministry where we were able to call many our family and friends.

That day, there was nothing particularly special to the schedule. My dad and I were sitting in the back; my wife and children were sitting with friends they had been catching up with before the service began. The worship was in full measure, people were engaged, and the

Lord was moving that morning. In a moment, the Lord spoke something to me that I never anticipated. It forever changed my perception of how I was agreeing with the prophetic. The Lord whispered, "You don't understand *faith* the way that I need you to know it."

Faith was one of those areas that I took a lot of pride in over the years. People are always calling huge steps "radical faith," and I was always the one exclaiming that "radical faith" was only obedience. The only reason it seems radical is because it goes against out flesh, but in reality it is nothing more than obedience. It was this mindset that drove me to take those steps in obedience. Throughout many decisions, I had earned a bit of a reputation that I was willing to take big risks of faith. Honestly, I thought I had mastered faith, and then the Lord busted my bubble.

I sat there in disbelief. How could I not understand faith? How could the Lord not recognize that my faith was strong and that I worked diligently to walk by faith and not by sight? The Lord had to be wrong. He had to have confused me with someone else, right? Prophetic dreams, visions, and words have been a part of my life for the majority of my life, and now it seemed that the Lord was calling me out on the one area that I had felt was structurally strong. What I did not understand in that moment was that the Lord was developing the prophetic by connecting the dots for me personally. We often hold the keys that unlock doors, but we find ourselves standing before unlocked doors that remain closed. The Lord was revealing the authority to open the unlocked doors.

Fast-forward three months—my family and I were ministering at a revival in Virginia when my cell phone rang. It was my mother. When I picked up the phone, I immediately heard her crying. "Ryan, this is your mom. I'm calling to tell you that I have cancer. The doctors say I have breast cancer."

What my mom didn't know at that very moment was that the Lord had been preparing me for this phone call. When He spoke to me on that first Sunday in January, He had taken me on a specific journey. For those three months, the Lord was teaching me about the prophetic and how we are to fight for the promises that come through dreams, visions, and/or prophetic words. The Lord had prepared me for this moment, and it was then that I realized that the cancer was an attempt from the enemy to prematurely take my mother from this world. The enemy had a plan, but the Lord gave me a strategy.

Little did I know that the strategy would help me give so many others the key that unlocks the door that is before them. With this key, you will unlock what is before you and the Lord will give you the authority to open doors to your destiny!

CHAPTER 1

WHAT WE THINK WE KNOW

"Faith is taking the first step even when you don't see the whole staircase."
—MARTIN LUTHER KING, JR,
as quoted in *Atlanta Magazine*, April 2008

Faith is one of those tricky topics. We feel like we know everything about faith, and yet it's often the topic that we know the least about. So many individuals will define faith as believing in something or someone. Some people grew up having faith in Santa Claus, the Easter bunny, or the tooth fairy. We grew up believing in these figures because we knew that if we denied their existence, it would be detrimental to our gift potential. The truth is that the majority of our faith is structured on this model. We are taught to believe in certain things or people in hopes that we will get something in return. The moment that we lose our faith, we begin to risk not getting what we feel like we deserve or should get just because we are who we are.

Whether voluntarily or involuntarily, we have developed our faith to be something that the Lord never intended it to be. Granted, we know the scriptures and we can often quote them verse by verse. That's not the challenge. The challenge is whether or not we can actually live by the standard of what the Word is actually saying. Not what we think that it says or what we want it to say—but what the Word of the Lord is really saying. We miss so much because we are easily swayed by our own flesh. In our weaknesses, we just do our best, and when we fail we create a concept of the Lord's Word that tells us we are doing good enough. We so desperately want to believe that when our faith fails us, the Lord is eagerly waiting to wink and nod with full understanding that we are mere mortals and He must be willing to turn His head and act like we never lacked in our faith.

WHAT BELIEF IS

From the very beginning of mankind, faith has always been a battle between what we know to be true and what we think we understand. We find ourselves in dire need, in circumstances that seem impossible to man, and in those moments we need the Lord to move in a way that we may have never seen or experienced before. The Lord begins saying things to us that make little to no sense within our natural minds. He reveals things to us, yet we fail to agree with His declarations because we need a tangible reality in the midst of our challenges. We think that our faith is a blueprint that builds us up spiritually to endure the test of time. We may not always understand the big picture or be able to see the entire structure, but we sincerely believe that we can live our life in faith because of the blueprint. But then there comes a day when we can no longer see the blueprint, and we are only given a dream, a vision, or a word through someone we barely know.

> *And without faith it is impossible to please Him,*
> *for he who comes to God must believe that He is*
> *and that He is a rewarder of those who seek Him*
> (Hebrews 11:6).

Hebrews 11:6 is the ultimate faith verse. It's the defining word on faith, the value of faith in our lives, and how it correlates with the Lord. All of us would eagerly say that we have faith in our lives. We would quickly explain how our faith in the Lord is what keeps us striving to be the best kind of "Christian" we can be. We tell ourselves that our faith must be maintained so that we will never be the person who fails to please the Lord. Each one of us wants to please the Lord.

However, a lack of faith is one of those things that we makes excuses for in the difficult times because it's just too hard, and surely God understands that I didn't have the faith to withstand that test. We write off our lack of faith, never questioning whether we have pleased the Lord. After all, we are just human, right? None of us are perfect, nor can we live a life without failures. Surely the Lord understands that some things are just more difficult and challenging to have faith for. Surely the Lord will view our weakness through the lens of humankind rather than through the lens of abiding in Christ.

The problem with this kind of thinking is that we never consider how faith may be the key to unlocking our prophetic destinies. We never make ourselves apply faith to the prophetic declarations in our lives. We have a dream, a vision, or a word that is steeped with a prophetic destiny for our life. We rarely consider the importance of applying faith to those words. We have the tendency to think that because we dreamed about it, had a vision for it, or someone prophesied it, those things will simply come to pass. We tell ourselves to agree and say amen so that we are connected to those words. When we have prophetic words revealed to us, we get so excited that

God is speaking that we fail to remember that there is an immediate spiritual battle engaged over those words. The enemy does not want to see the prophetic fulfilled in our lives. The enemy wants to see those words fail to reach full maturation. He celebrates our failures as we unwillingly help the enemy keep those words from maturing.

It's amazing how many times we have prophetic dreams but never write them down. We wake up, ponder those events, and then quickly move on with our day. We go about our daily lives, and suddenly we encounter a supernatural vision that alters our moment in time, yet we treat it the same as the dream. Just a moment in time. We attend our church services or special events and have a guest who receives a word of knowledge or has a prophetic word directly to us. We get excited, but like the dreams and visions, we go home with no intention of connecting those words with our destiny. I hear so many people talk about how they put those words on the shelf until they come to fruition. Truth is, we place them on the "hypothetical shelf," never to remember them except at the moment we feel like the Lord has failed to come through with what He promised to do.

We get angry with the Lord. We get frustrated, believing that the Lord lied or somehow is punishing us for our failures. We exclaim how we are hurting, and how could the Lord not move on our behalf? We think that we know how the prophetic works, and yet we fail to see the prophetic fulfilled. How could the Lord make these prophetic declarations and then permit our lives to be a constant shadow of failure after failure? Does the Lord not care about whether or not the dreams come true? Why would He give us these visions only to never see them become reality? It had to have been a false prophet, or they were prophesying out of their flesh. These are the questions that we find ourselves asking. Yet we never ask ourselves whether or not we did our part in the fulfillment of the promises. It's always easier to blame others when we aren't willing to look at our own lives. We need someone or something to blame, but we can't be the ones who missed it.

Of course, we are quick to say that we receive these words or declarations, which means we are saying that we believe them, to an extent. But that's where it all stops. We say we believe, but do we really? Believing in something and having faith for something are two different things.

Let's take a look at the definitions of these two terms in Hebrews 11.

> *And without **faith** it is impossible to please Him, for he who comes to God must **believe** that He is and that He is a rewarder of those who seek Him* (Hebrews 11:6).

Faith (*pistis*): persuasion, credence; moral conviction (of religious truth, or the truthfulness of God or a religious teacher), especially reliance upon Christ for salvation; abstractly, constancy in such profession; by extension, the system of religious (Gospel) truth itself: assurance (Strong's #G4102).

Believe (*pisteuo*): to have faith (in, upon, or with respect to, a person or thing), credits, by implication, to en*trust* (especially one's spiritual well-being to Christ), commit (to trust), put *trust* in (Strong's #G4100).

When we look at the meaning of these two words, we find similarities in their definitions, and yet we also find distinctions. One of those distinctions is that the word *believe* is connected to *trust*. So many times we want to have faith in people, but we are hindered because the person has failed us before. With that in mind, we recognize that it's not that we simply don't have faith in them, but we are struggling to connect that faith with trust. Let me say it this way: we will be quick to say that we have faith in the Lord for our lives, but do we trust Him with our lives? Oh, I know that many will quickly respond that they trust the Lord, but their lives rarely reveal that trust.

We think that faith has the ability to stand alone, and because of that thought we have convinced ourselves that faith is nothing more than believing in the Lord. We rarely connect faith with trust and sincere belief with faith. We have an equation. We believe that Jesus is the Son of God, He died for our sins, and He was raised from death unto life so that we may receive Him as our Savior—and we call that faith. Occasionally we make the statement that we have "faith to overcome" or maybe the "faith to believe" for something that we are anticipating. I get it, and I am in no way implying that people are wrong to make those kinds of statements, because they are true. I am saying that we don't understand how faith really works.

How can this be? It is because we have made faith into the Santa Claus formula—believe in X in order to get Y. Many have inadvertently made prophetic promises following this pattern. If we don't believe or have faith in the promises (Santa Claus) then they won't come true. So we naturally say we believe the prophecy, and that's that. When we live the life of faith in this manner, we have a problem, because sometimes we see promises fulfilled and sometimes we don't. Why? We said we believed the word, right? Without realizing it, we start to feel like God is either good or bad based on whether or not the promises were fulfilled. We make His goodness and faithfulness conditional. We don't ask ourselves if we have done our part and cultivated those promises by trusting in the Lord with our lives or walking the promise out in faith. We forget that God cannot lie.

WHAT UNBELIEF IS

In Mark 9, we find the story of a father longing for help concerning his son who is being tormented by a demonic spirit. The scriptures tell us how the demon spirit would throw this child into the fire in order to burn him alive. The demonic spirit would not stop there but would throw the young boy into the water in an effort to drown him. The torment resembled what we now would call epileptic seizures. This demonic spirit was vicious, causing the boy to foam at the mouth and gnash his teeth, and causing his body to become stiff as a board.

The father attempted to help his son by bringing him to the disciples. Unfortunately for the father, at that time the disciples were not strong enough to deliver the boy from the demonic spirit. The father made a desperate plea to Jesus for His help concerning his son. It's at this moment we see one of the more peculiar ways that Jesus could have responded to the father. Jesus addressed the father and the crowd that was gathered by calling them a "faithless generation." Then Jesus asked the question, "How long shall I be with you?" Jesus was literally asking how long should He put up with this faithless generation. At this point, Jesus does not sound like He cares for the boy, the father, and potentially the crowd. Honestly, in today's culture this is where an overwhelming majority would have gotten offended and walked out on Jesus.

Think about how this response would have caused many today to get mad at what appeared to be a lack of love from Jesus. Here is this father, hurting and in desperation for his son, pleading for Jesus to help him. And yet Jesus calls him faithless and ask how much longer He should put up with him.

It's easy to take offense in the midst of our battles. It's easy to be hurt by others when we are already hurting emotionally, mentally, and/or spiritually. However, do we take the time to consider what Jesus was trying to say to the father and the crowd? Do we take the time in the midst of our greatest trials to understand what others are saying to us? Or do we simply look for the answer to our problem without recognizing the challenge to see God (the Father) at work in us? Though it first appears that Jesus is being offensive toward the father, He is actually about to reveal what the father is capable of within himself.

When the boy was brought to Jesus, He immediately saw how the demonic spirit was tormenting the boy. Jesus asked the father how long it had been occurring, and the father told Jesus that this had been happening since he was a little child. Then, Jesus gave the father something to realize in his own life. Jesus said to the father, "If you can believe, all things are possible to those who believe." The father quickly responded with a statement that we have repeated many times throughout the years: "I do believe, but help my unbelief."

> *Immediately the boy's father cried out and said,*
> ***"I do believe; help my unbelief"*** (Mark 9:24).

That single verse has been used by so many who are struggling with faith. We use it as an opportunity to acknowledge unbelief in our lives. Like the father, we quickly declare that we believe, yet as soon as we say that we often quickly follow it up with the acknowledgment that we also have unbelief. "I do believe; help my unbelief" has become such a prominent statement in our Christian language. Unbelief has become like a rite of passage allowing us to live our lives being okay with not having enough faith. We sincerely believe that if we admit our struggle in the area of lacking in faith, somehow God will wink and be okay with that.

We know from scripture that every person is given a measure of faith (see Rom. 12:3). That presents a very challenging problem for us. We can all agree that we have been given this measure of faith, but it would appear at times that the faith of others is greater than our own. Does the Lord give more "measure" to someone else and your measure is limited? That word *measure* is *metron* (Strong's #G3358); it means a limited portion. Over the years I have come to understand that the "measure" of faith that is being spoken of here is what the Lord gives every person so that humankind will be able to one day connect their faith with the reality that Jesus is the Son of God. That measure of faith is enough to help us believe in Jesus, that He came to this world, died, and was resurrected for us. God positioned faith to already be activated within us.

Here lies the problem. We begin to tell ourselves that unbelief means that we believe partially, but that's okay because we are limited in our ability to fully believe. We had faith, just not enough faith; therefore the Lord understands our "unbelief." When we tell the Lord that we have unbelief, we are ultimately saying that we believe but our faith is weak and it's not where it should be.

Sadly, we have convinced ourselves that unbelief is okay. There is irony in telling ourselves that somehow God is okay with a lack of faith. Consider the times that Jesus rebuked the disciples for a lack of faith, and then ask yourself: "How do I get a pass and they did not?" Strangely, we have convinced ourselves that somehow the Lord is not displeased with us. We know Hebrews 11:6, *"And without faith it is impossible to please Him, for he who comes to God must believe that He is and that He is a rewarder of those who seek Him,"* yet we are quick to explain away our limited faith because of unbelief. Did we ever stop to ask ourselves if we are wrong, though? What if we have spent years acting like a lack of faith is something that God just winks at (after all, we are just humans), and we have created an excuse because we aren't willing to trust the Lord?

> Unbelief (*apaistia*): faithlessness, (negatively) disbelief (lack of Christian faith), or (positively) unfaithfulness (disobedience) (Strong's #G570).

Looking at this particular definition should shake us up because part of the meaning of unbelief is *disobedience*. And yet, it doesn't seem like it's enough to help us overcome our unwillingness to walk in faith. What's interesting is that this word *apaistia* is actually from another Greek word, *apistos* (Strong's #G571). This word means *untrustworthy*. It's important that we get this because it reveals to us that the father of the epileptic boy was telling Jesus that he believed that Jesus could heal his son, but he did not *trust* Jesus enough to heal him. He may have lacked trust because of the disciples' earlier failure; even so, we have to see the true meaning behind the statement of unbelief.

Please allow me to reiterate the importance of what I am saying about "unbelief" and how we use it. When we determine that having little to no faith is okay with God, we just make ourselves feel better about our circumstances or situations. I recognize that there will always be times in our lives when we may struggle in our faith. When we are greatly tested in the midst of a storm, our faith can become weak and even seem as though it is not there. This should be why we reach out to the Lord for help and reach out to our brothers and sisters in Christ who can pray for us and with us. The beauty of the family of God is that we are not required to walk this alone. We call upon the Lord and we call upon others who can help strengthen us in our weakest moments.

> *Trust in the Lord with all your heart and do not lean on your own understanding. In all your ways acknowledge Him, and He will make your paths straight* (Proverbs 3:5-6).

> *Trust in the Lord completely, and do not rely on your own opinions. With all your heart rely on him to guide you, and he will lead you in every decision you make. Become intimate with him in whatever you do, and he will lead you wherever you go. Don't think for a moment that you know it all* (Proverbs 3:5-7 TPT).

We need to recognize that the root of our problem with faith is often our inability to *trust in the Lord*. We say that we have faith in prophetic dreams, visions, and/or words from the Lord. Yet many times our hinderance is not a lack of faith; we just don't trust the Lord to see the promises fulfilled. We fail to have faith in the Lord because we aren't willing to trust Him with the process of fulfillment. What we think we know is often not what we know at all.

CHAPTER 2

WHAT FAITH IS

*"I now had enough faith not only to
believe there were answer [sic], but to feel
certain that those answers would become
apparent at some point in the future."*
—BEN CARSON, *Take the Risk*

According to *Vine's Expository Dictionary of New Testament Words*, the word *faith* means, primarily, "firm persuasion," a conviction based upon hearing (akin to *peitho*, "to persuade"), and it is used in the New Testament always of "faith in God or Christ, or things spiritual." Faith in the invisible God is distinct from "faith" in man; it is a firm conviction, producing a full acknowledgement of God's revelation or truth.

DEFINING FAITH

Paul wrote to the Romans to explain what faith should look like for us when we are in right relationship with the Lord.

> [Jesus,] *whom God displayed publicly as a propitiation in His blood through* **faith**. *This was to demonstrate His righteousness, because in the forbearance of God He passed over the sins previously committed* (Romans 3:25).

Look closely at what Paul says to the church at Corinth. His preaching of Christ was to develop their faith and was not dependent upon men.

> *And when I came to you, brethren, I did not come with superiority of speech or of wisdom, proclaiming to you the testimony of God. For I determined to know nothing among you except Jesus Christ, and Him crucified. I was with you in weakness and in fear and in much trembling, and my message and my preaching were not in persuasive words of wisdom, but in demonstration of the Spirit and of power, so that your faith would not rest on the wisdom of men, but on the power of God* (1 Corinthians 2:1-5).

Why is this so important? Look at how Paul addresses the Corinthians with the understanding of our faith in

Christ. Paul reminds the Corinthians of the worth of their faith in Christ. If there is no faith, there is no resurrection to recognize.

> *Now if Christ is preached, that He has been raised from the dead, how do some among you say that there is no resurrection of the dead? But if there is no resurrection of the dead, not even Christ has been raised; and if Christ has not been raised, then our preaching is vain, your faith also is vain. Moreover we are even found to be false witnesses of God, because we testified against God that He raised Christ, whom He did not raise, if in fact the dead are not raised. For if the dead are not raised, not even Christ has been raised; and if Christ has not been raised, your faith is worthless; you are still in your sins* (1 Corinthians 15:12-17).

If I were to ask you, "What is faith?" many would respond with Hebrews 11:1: *"Now faith is the substance of things hoped for, the evidence of things not seen"* (NKJV). But can you explain, with understanding, what faith is? Okay, I will admit that this point may be a bit confusing if you read over this quickly.

Here are the facts:

1. Faith is the substance of things hoped for.

2. Faith is the evidence of things not yet seen.

So faith is believing in something (or someone) that you are hoping for but not yet able to see. How can we activate our faith to believe and trust in order to see prophetic promises fulfilled? We have the definitions and the knowledge about faith, but do we have faith being demonstrated in our lives? In other words, are we trusting in the Lord? When He gives us a prophetic word, whether through dreams, visions, or prophecy, is the substance of our faith enough? Does the substance provide the evidence even though we have yet to see the fulfillment of the promise? When we live our lives trying to determine what faith is, we miss the point of living out our faith.

Personally, I love how *The Passion Translation* handles this particular verse:

> *Now faith brings our hopes into reality and becomes the foundation needed to acquire the things we long for. It is all the evidence required to prove what is still unseen* (Hebrews 11:1 TPT).

I love this because it reminds you and me that faith brings hope into our reality. Faith becomes a foundation that establishes all the evidence we need when we cannot yet see the things we long for. Faith is our activation. Faith is not a dormant life; it is not unworthy begging and pleading with the Lord in the midst of trials. Faith is more than a glimpse of believing that Someone exists.

Faith Is Active

Look at the life of Noah. He had not seen the evidence of a flood, much less rain, yet he activated his faith in the Lord by building an ark. Although the Lord had spoken to Noah, he had to apply the word in faith and build something that no one had ever seen or could describe. Noah had to pick up a hammer!

Faith Is Responsible

As a son or daughter of God it is our responsibility to be faithful to obey God's Word and apply His Word in our calling by loving and serving one another. How could we, being sons of God, refuse to obey His Word responsibly in faith?

Faith Is Foundational

Faith is our personal foundation upon which we build our relationship with the Lord. When we experience the disappointments and pain in life, there is a foundation we stand on, knowing that God has proven His unfailing trustworthiness again and again.

Faith Is Pure

Pure faith rightly reflects God's truth. Impure faith contains falsehood and needs to be refined with fire (see 1 Pet. 1:7). The way to keep faith pure is to eliminate the opinions of man and place everything in the hands of the Lord.

Faith Is Relational

Faith develops in our personal growth as we get to know God more and more. Faith does not only come by the written Word; there has to be a relational application in our lives. When we receive the Word for ourselves, faith not only comes into our minds, but it comes alive in our hearts.

Faith Is Genuine

When we are in Christ, He works to conform us to His image. That transformation is the evidence of faith displayed in our character, our integrity, the way we conduct ourselves, and in our conversation. It is not of our own selves. Jesus said that ultimately the proof would be revealed in our obedience to Word of God.

Faith Is Revelatory

At the moment that Abraham took the knife to fulfill the word of the Lord and take Isaac's life, the Lord revealed a ram caught in the thicket for the sacrifice. There, in that moment, because of Abraham's faith it was revealed to him that God was a Provider. We see this pattern throughout the Bible. When individuals place their faith in the Lord, there is a pivotal moment in which they receive revelation about the Father.

Faith Is Confident

Faith has an "I just know it to be true" mentality that rises within you and accepts the reality that what God has said is as good as done. Faith gives us confidence, in our present moments, of the truth of what God has already said concerning our future.

Faith Is Trustworthy

Throughout the ministry of Christ, He kept telling the disciples that He would go to Jerusalem to die, be buried, and rise from the dead on the third day. That was difficult to put their faith in; they needed to apply trust to the words of Christ. The moment that Mary came back declaring that the body was no longer in the tomb, she demonstrated her willingness to trust through faith.

Faith Is Our Key to Unlocking the Prophetic Promises of Our Lives

With every promise there is a challenge to apply faith so that we will not waver in our journey to see it fulfilled. Keys never truly open doors; they only unlock them. You have to push or pull that door to see it open. Likewise, when there is a prophetic promise given to you, faith will be the key to unlock the door spiritually, but you must open that door with a push or a pull (activation).

APPLIED FAITH

At this point, if I were to ask you to give a personal understanding of what faith is, how would you describe it? Could you articulate what faith is? You may be surprised how difficult it is to come up with a simple definition. We have been a generation who defines faith as believing, but we don't know how to demonstrate the fullness of faith and please the Lord. We understand that faith is necessary for our salvation, but the moment that we recognize that faith should be applied to the prophetic, we rationalize why we don't have faith or why we are willing to live with unbelief (remember the meaning of unbelief from Chapter 1).

> *For in it the righteousness of God is revealed from faith to faith; as it is written, "But the righteous man shall live by faith"* (Romans 1:17).

We read passages like Romans 1:17, and we know we need to apply this in every aspect of our lives. You may be asking God to help you be better person. You may be seeking for wisdom, knowledge, or understanding with a certain problem. You may be asking the Lord to intervene at work concerning a problem. Maybe you are asking

God to help you with your finances. Maybe you need an advance on your salary or a promotion at work. Situations like these require faith, and we believe that if we serve the Lord He will respond on our behalf. We can all agree that these are principles and applications of faith.

Where it gets difficult and often overwhelming is in the big stuff. When we are believing for God to intervene in our marriage. When we are asking the Lord to convict our sons or daughters who may be away from the Lord. We struggle with believing that God can break our strongholds and addictions. Honestly, it's easier to believe for the things we consider minor; having faith in the difficult aspects of lives is challenging for us all. If we are real with ourselves, at times we can have more faith for others than we can for our own lives. It is often easier to believe that we will see something happen in our neighbors' lives than it is to have faith for the same thing in our own lives.

It's the flesh versus the Spirit. When the doctor gives you a bad report, often the first thing to go out the door is faith. Our flesh is quickly overwhelmed in the moment of bad news. I am not implying that people don't stand strong in the midst of bad news; I am stating that the majority of individuals come up against their biggest challenges in life unprepared, with a faith that could easily be called weak.

When we are facing difficult news, faith is a major challenge. It's so simple to tell others how to live their lives, but when it's our turn the walk is full of doubt and fear. That's why Hebrews 11 is really a fascinating passage of scripture. We have come to know this chapter as the Hall of Faith. With individual glimpses of men and women throughout the Word of God, Hebrews 11 gives us an idea of how these individuals embraced faith in their lives. They were against all odds, but they rose above their circumstances to see the Lord work on their behalf. We have long admired these individuals, placing them on an unattainable platform. We tell ourselves that if we had the faith of Abraham, or the faith of Noah, maybe the faith of Rahab, we too would be considered to be strong in faith.

It's funny how we read this chapter but fail to see what it really says. We are so convinced that when the Lord prophetically promised these individuals specific things, we believe that they saw them fulfilled. We believe that faith is seeing the prophetic fulfilled within our lifetime—yet faith has nothing to do with our own gratification. We have to be willing to see our faith as welcoming the prophetic promises on our lives from a distance.

I know what you're thinking. No one wants to see something from a distance, so far away that we never get to experience the fulfillment of those promises. We all want to see the end we hope for. No parent praying for their child to be delivered from drugs and living for the Lord wants to leave this world without seeing that child delivered and saved within the parent's lifetime. It's why we have our heroes of faith throughout the Bible. We admire their lives and great faith. We desire to walk with the kind of faith that each one of those heroes walked in. But what if I told you that these heroes we admire so much never saw the fulfillment of their promises in their own lifetime?

> *All these died in faith, without receiving the promises, but having seen them and having welcomed them from a distance, and having confessed that they were strangers and exiles on the earth* (Hebrews 11:13).

> *And all these, having gained approval through their faith, did not receive what was promised, because God had provided something better for us, so that apart from us they would not be made perfect* (Hebrews 11:39-40).

Faith is the ability to see something (not yet seen) from a distance so that we will live our lives in a way that we know (evidence) that God is going to fulfill His promises because He is not a liar (trust). But we all desire to see the fulfillment of what the Lord reveals to us. Whether it is in a dream, through a vision, or a word by an individual, we all want to see the word unveiled in its fullness. We want to see it fulfilled!

I don't want to discourage you at all. I want you to know that there will be many prophetic words that will be fulfilled in your lifetime. There will be dreams you see come true, visions manifested, and words that mature in ways that bring glory and honor to the Lord. Those fulfillments often will keep us encouraged and going strong. We will remember when the Lord spoke something and came through. We can remind of ourselves of those times and continue to keep going in remembrance of what the Lord did. When those promises develop for us, we have to use them as markers of remembrance for the promises that have yet to be. In other words, when the Lord has fulfilled promises in your life, then faith should rise up within you to know that what has not yet happened will still definitely come.

What do we do when we read verses like Hebrews 11:13 and 11:39, which specifically state that these heroes of faith never saw the fulfillment of their promises? Will there be times when the Lord will stretch our faith in the prophetic, ultimately having us step into eternity without receiving our promises? It doesn't seem right or fair. How could the Lord do such a thing to us when we desperately want to see the fulfillment of our "thus saith the Lord" moments? Is God punishing us for some hidden sin in our lives that we haven't dealt with? Is this some kind of mental game that the Lord is using against us?

Honestly, it has never been about seeing the prophetic fulfilled in our own lifetimes, even though that is how we would prefer it. If you are believing for a son or daughter to be delivered from drugs and receive Christ as their Savior, you most definitely want to see that happen before you step into eternity. There is nothing wrong with having a strong desire to see your child come to the Lord.

God is more than capable of giving you a prophetic dream, vision, or word that your child will be delivered and will serve the Lord, but that promise could happen after you are no longer here. Again, why would the Lord give you a word but not allow you to see the fulfillment in your lifetime? Let's look at this question in a different form. Why do we feel that a promise is validated as real only if we see it happen? Why do we determine whether prophecy is accurate by the fulfillment? Now, I know that is a dangerous question, but I ask it because there have been many prophetic words spoken, but time had to pass before those words were fulfilled.

Think of Isaiah at the moment when he prophesied about the Messiah in Isaiah 53. Isaiah detailed an event in time that no one could yet fully comprehend nor imagine. He began the chapter with the question, *"Who has believed our message?"* (I find it very interesting that he begins his passage describing future events by asking whether or not we believe.) Isaiah then prophesies about a man who would not stand out or draw people to Him by His appearance. It would be the complete opposite—this man would be despised, rejected, one of many sorrows, someone who would be no stranger to suffering and grief during His lifetime. If that's not difficult enough to imagine, Isaiah then goes into detail about this man carrying our sickness and being willing to endure the torment of our suffering. God will strike Him low because of our rebellion. His flesh would be pierced because of the works of mankind, and as a result of our sins this man would be crushed. Isaiah goes on to describe the punishment He endured to help make us whole. In the prophecy, Isaiah described actions of man with the analogy of sheep. Likewise, he used a lamb being led to the slaughter to identify the torment this man would experience.

Could you imagine hearing this prophecy and trying to understand what Isaiah was saying? Not only that, think about the moment when Isaiah said that it pleased God to bring this crushing and grief upon this man. That doesn't sound very loving! Yet Isaiah goes on to reveal the purpose of glory behind the pain and suffering the Messiah would one day endure. There was a bigger picture to the prophecy.

Prophecy released—now, Lord, do Your job and see this fulfilled. The days passed, the weeks turned into months, and months into years. It would be approximately 700 years from the life of Isaiah until the fulfillment of what he prophesied about the Son of God, Jesus. Imagine the ridicule that may have come as each passing day went by without a glimpse of hope to see these words come true. Imagine having such a strong and powerful word concerning the Savior of the world—but no evidence in your lifetime. Nothing to confirm or acknowledge that you were right in the prophecy. If this happened in our day, the multitudes would have already defined Isaiah as a false prophet (sadly, most don't know what a false prophet scripturally is). My goodness, there had to be days when Isaiah longed to see the man he described, but he never saw any of this fulfilled in his own lifetime. Honestly, how did Isaiah not struggle or want to give up hoping for such a man?

This is where we have to understand that although Isaiah never saw the prophecy fulfilled in the natural in his lifetime, he actually did see it—from a distance. This is your key—Isaiah saw it! Granted, he never saw with his natural eyes, but he welcomed it through his spiritual eyes. He knew because he not only heard the Lord, he could see the prophecy being fulfilled.

Here is where faith gets us. Remember that our faith is not just about believing, but it's also about being connected with trust. We have to first learn how to trust the Lord when we receive these prophetic declarations. Demanding that the Lord make this happen in our lifetime or it's not real is the number-one reason our faith is limited. We have to get to the place in our lives where our faith is so strong that when prophetic dreams, visions, and words come to us, we believe, trust, and demonstrate that our faith is in the Lord—whether or not we see it. The truth is, you have seen it!

Go back and read those verses found in Hebrews 11. Notice that they "saw and welcomed them from a distance." You and I have to understand that our dreams, visions, and words exist because the Lord is showing us His reality. It's difficult to accept at times, but it might just be that it's not entirely about you! The Lord is revealing His promises to you—it's a privilege! God is not punishing you by withholding the fulfillment in your lifetime. The Lord isn't angry with you and therefore determining to only give you a glimpse of something but never actually let you see it. If you are able to recognize the promise, your responsibility is to align yourself in faith with the reality that God cannot lie. That means that whether you get to see it or not, it's going to come to pass.

God is not a man, that He should lie, nor a son of man, that He should repent; has He said, and will He not do it? Or has He spoken, and will He not make it good? (Numbers 23:19)

We have to learn how to live out the story of our lives knowing that the promise has already been declared fulfilled. I get it—it's still difficult to live it out. It's overwhelming when you feel like it's never going to happen. It's hard to believe that God is showing us later parts of our lives to get us to live by faith, yet there is a chance that we may not be able to see these things come to pass.

If faith is like this, what about Abraham? After all, he is described as the father of our faith. Why does the faith of Abraham seem so superior to our own? Did he have the secret to what faith is?

CHAPTER 3

THE FATHER OF IT ALL

"When God tempted or tried Abraham with that difficult command of offering up his son, it was not for His satisfaction, whether he feared God or no, but for Abraham's own greater satisfaction and comfort, and the more clear manifestation of the favour of God to him."
—JONATHAN EDWARDS,
A Treatise Concerning Religious Affections

I remember as a child visiting a church for vacation Bible school and singing those songs about Father Abraham and his many sons. I remember hearing the stories of how Abraham had this great faith that he demonstrated in his life. Many can recall those songs and the stories of

Abraham that were told to us at a child's level. There's nothing wrong with the songs or the stories, but a problem develops when we grow up and never read the Word for ourselves. We develop a mental picture of how Abraham never wavered in his faith, and over time as we admire his life we end up limiting ours in comparison.

Abraham is only a small example; we have lived in comparison with many others throughout the Bible. We often live in the shadows of these men and women, telling ourselves, "If we could only be more like them." The truth is, they all had their many faults. They all made their mistakes and made horrible decisions along the way. We admire them but often fail to actually model our lives after the one who matters the most—Jesus. We put Jesus on the unattainable platform and settle for other role models we believe are more attainable. When it comes to faith, we go over and over Hebrews 11, longing to be more and more like these men and women of great faith. We rarely take the time to look over their lives to see that they were just like you and me. Yes, David was a man after God's own heart (see 1 Sam. 13:14; Acts 13:22), but he was also a man who executed a plan to have another woman's husband murdered on the battlefield (see 2 Sam. 11–12).

But let's look at the life of old Father Abraham. After all, he is often called the father of our faith. For years, I simply thought that the reason Abraham had earned this title was because he had said *yes*. I was so convinced that he became this great man of faith because of his yes. Was I wrong? Not necessarily; our faith is increased over time when we learn how to say *yes* to the Lord. Could it be that simple? Could he have become this great man of faith just because of a yes? What I have learned is that it was more than that. So much more!

Paul said, *"For what does the Scripture say? 'Abraham believed God, and it was credited to him as righteousness'"* (Rom. 4:3). And James said, *"And the Scripture was fulfilled which says, 'And Abraham believed God, and it was reckoned to him as righteousness,' and he was called the friend of God"* (James 2:23).

Paul would say that all believers were the children of Abraham: *"Therefore know that only those who are of faith are sons of Abraham"* (Gal. 3:7 NKJV). Look at how the Lord personally spoke to Abraham and addressed not only his day, but many generations that would follow thereafter.

> *Then behold, the word of the Lord came to him, saying, "This man will not be your heir; but one who will come forth from your own body, he shall be your heir." And He took him outside and said, "Now look toward the heavens, and count the stars, if you are able to count them." And He said to him, "So shall your descendants*

be." Then he believed in the Lord; and He reckoned it to him as righteousness (Genesis 15:4-6).

No one from the Old Testament is mentioned more often throughout the New Testament than Abraham. The impact that he made during his life was profound, lasting beyond the days he spent as a man on the earth. When we study the life of Abraham, we learn a lot about him, but in reality we know very little about him before the time we are first introduced to him in Genesis 11. Abraham's father, Terah, lived in Ur. Ur was a very influential city in the southern part of Mesopotamia between the Euphrates River and the Persian Gulf. We do know that Terah was an idol worshiper who began to take his family to the land of Canaan, but he never made it there. Instead, they ended up settling in the city of Haran. Abraham's family history is not one of great faith in the Lord; his foundation is one built on the worshiping of false gods.

Although Abraham's family were idol worshipers, the Lord had a plan greater than false gods for his life. We see this in Genesis:

Now the Lord said to Abram, "Go forth from your country, and from your relatives and from your father's house, to the land which I will show you; and I will make you a great nation, and I will bless you, and make your name great; and so you shall be a blessing; and I will bless those who bless you, and the one who curses you I will curse. And in you all the families of the earth will be blessed." So Abram went forth as the Lord had spoken to him; and Lot went with him. Now Abram was seventy-five years old when he departed from Haran (Genesis 12:1-4).

God called Abraham to leave his home and told him to go to a land that He would show to him. Imagine Abraham coming home to Sarah and telling her that the Lord had spoken to him and told him to leave their home, don't take anything with them except a few items, and bring no family as well. What was the response of Sarah when she heard this? Did she tell him to go back and listen more intently to the Lord? Did she try to tell Abraham to be reasonable and have some common sense because there was no way that the Lord would say to go without giving accurate directions? Did she or Abraham try to rationalize out of being obedient to the Lord? I mean, seriously, think about the fact that Abraham had no directions other than the guidance from the Lord. In the process the Lord also made three direct promises to Abraham:

1. Abraham would have land of his own.

2. Abraham would be made into a great nation.

3.   Abraham would become a great blessing.

I have always felt that Abraham was called the father of our faith because of his yes in Genesis 12:4. It's the pivotal moment when Abraham responded quickly to the call of the Lord. It appears to us that he did so without hesitation and left everything and everyone behind. Imagine that kind of faith. The faith to obey the Lord by leaving everything behind, not knowing where you are going. It's this kind of faith that causes us to put Abraham on the platform that we feel like we can't obtain. Many of us want to be obedient to what the Lord is calling us to do, but the truth is that we limit ourselves because we want everything laid out before us. Once we see the entire blueprint, we will consider whether or not we say yes or no.

HEARING FROM GOD

I remember sitting in the office of a pastor—a personal friend for years—discussing the struggle of obedience to what the Lord was calling him to do. He was overseeing a very large congregation, what many would define as a megachurch, and the challenges before him could be intimidating. He looked at me and said, "Ryan, I have always admired your faith. Your willingness to go and do whatever the Lord says is something I respect. You don't seem to hesitate or waver in your yes. Your faith is so encouraging to me. Your faith is so radical."

At that moment I remember looking at this guy and saying, "There is no such thing as radical faith. 'Radical faith' is simply *yes* to obedience. It only appears to be radical because it goes against our flesh and everything we know to be common or make sense."

This pastor then said something that forever changed my understanding of how many people determine to be obedient to the Lord in faith. "Ryan, I cannot say yes until I see everything laid out before me. I have to see how it is going to work before I will ever consider it to have my yes."

I looked at this pastor, responding with a direct word: "That's not faith!"

He answered, "I know, but I am just telling you that I have to see it as it is before I can say yes."

In that moment, I recognized that this pastor wasn't alone in his process of yes to the Lord. I hear so many people talk about how they have to see everything before them in order to consider whether or not they say yes. In other words, many individuals have to see every single detail. Everything that they may lose or gain if they say yes to the Lord. This mentality has limited us in so many areas because we want the Lord to show us every step in the direction that He is guiding us. If it gets too difficult or challenging, we will quickly tap out.

LEARN TO FIGHT THE GOOD FIGHT

This charge I commit to you, son Timothy, according to the prophecies previously made concerning you, that by them you may wage the good warfare, having faith and a good conscience, which some having rejected (1 Timothy 1:18-19 NKJV).

Many are just like that pastor. What would Abraham really have said if God laid out his life before him? Would he still have said yes?

Imagine the Lord sits Abraham down and says, "Abraham, I am going to make you the father of many. I want you to say yes to me. Will you say yes?"

Maybe in that moment Abraham looks up to the Lord and says, "Well, before I can say yes or no, I am going to need You to tell me everything that will be involved."

So the Lord agrees. Take a little trip with me on my imagination; it's going to be a fun ride.

THE CONVERSATION

God: "Abraham, I am going to make you great and bless your name. You will become a father at an impossible time in your life. Your wife will actually laugh at the notion of becoming pregnant so late in life. As a matter of fact, she will give up and tell you to sleep with her handmaiden in order to conceive a child. Abraham, you being the husband you are and wanting to make your wife happy, you'll agree to sleep with the handmaiden. Unfortunately, this will not make your wife happy and she eventually has you run the handmaiden off with the child you both conceived. By the way, Abraham, his name will be Ishmael. Time will pass, but eventually you and your wife Sarah will conceive a child named Isaac. This child is the destiny of the promises of your life. But at a certain time I will ask you to sacrifice the child."

Abraham: "Wait a minute. Wait one minute. You're telling me that the child who is a key to the promises that You spoke into my life, that child, You're telling me that I am going to sacrifice the promise?"

God: "I know it sounds crazy, doesn't it? But be patient, Abraham; it gets better. You won't have to sacrifice the promise as there will be a ram caught in the thicket to replace your son. Over time that young man will mature and grow up to a point where he desires a wife. It will be a very interesting process as Isaac will eventually find a wife in exchange for nine camels. It will turn out to be a decent deal. Rebekah will soon become pregnant with twins in her womb. There the twins will already be fighting one another. Eventually one will be birthed first, full of red hair, and the second will be known as a heel catcher and deceiver. Jacob will be a trickster and Esau will be a hunter. One day Esau will give up his birthright as the firstborn for a cup of soup. Abraham, can you believe that your grandson will give up his birthright over a bowl of soup? Nevertheless, Jacob will begin the process of taking on the identity of Esau with the help of his mother to deceive Isaac for the blessing of the firstborn son. The deception will work as Isaac is weak in his eyes and hearing. Once Esau discovers what happened he will pursue Jacob and Jacob will have to flee from his brother. There will come a time when I will have to wrestle with Jacob. I will dislocate his hip, and he will no longer be known as the trickster or deceiver, for I will rename him Israel.

"Eventually Jacob will have twelve sons. Those twelve sons will one day become the twelve tribes of Israel, but before then there will be one known as Joseph. Joseph will be a dreamer—so much a dreamer that he doesn't know when to keep his mouth shut at times. Joseph will be the favorite of his father, and because of the favoritism and his dreams, jealousy will rise within his brothers. The brothers one day will beat Joseph and throw him into a pit. They will rip the coat that their father made for Joseph as they lie to their father and tell him that Joseph is dead. Joseph will become a slave to the Ishmaelites. Look, Abraham, the people who will put your great-grandson into slavery will be the very people you gave birth to—Ishmael."

Abraham: "Stop! You can't expect me to say yes to something like this."

God: "Abraham, just be patient, it gets better. From the pit to slavery, Joseph eventually will end up in Egypt where the wife of Potiphar will lie and claim that he attempted to sleep with her, which will land Joseph in prison. There Joseph will remain for years, but he will have a glimpse of hope as he reveals the dreams of a baker and a cupbearer. Eventually, Joseph will be released from prison and placed second in command over all of Egypt. There his brothers will return, not knowing who Joseph is, but after putting them through tests Joseph will reveal his identity and once again be reunited with his father.

"Sadly for the twelve tribes, they will enter into bondage in Egypt. They will become slaves for hundreds of years. Eventually, I will raise up a child in the Egyptian household by the name of Moses. Moses will be raised Egyptian, but he will be Hebrew through your great-grandson Levi. Moses will be the deliverer of the Israelites, and he will eventually become the pastor of the church of whiners, moaners, and complainers. Moses will do good, but he's no Charlton Heston (laugh people, it's all a part of my imagination). Moses will establish a place where I can visit the people, and as I visit with Moses there will be a man named Joshua who will be drawn to the glory. Moses will be unable to lead the children of Israel into the promised land because he will have a real bad temper. It's why I will raise Joshua to lead them. Joshua will eventually send spies into the city of Jericho, and there they will meet Rahab, the harlot, who will help them. Rahab will join the tribes of Israel and she will marry a man by the name of Salmon. They will have a child named Boaz. Boaz will have a son named Jesse, and Jesse will eventually have a son name David.

"David will be a shepherd boy whom I will anoint to be king because the people want a king. Before David will be king I will give them one called Saul. Saul will be evil in his ways, while David will be a man after My own heart. David will kill a bear and a lion with his hands. He will cut off the head of giants, and he will be a mighty warrior of Saul. However, David will also have blood on his hands as he will commit adultery and lose a child due to the nature of his sin. David will eventually repent for the sin of adultery. He will thereafter have a son called Solomon who will build a temple to host My presence. Solomon will be wise, but he will also make mistakes. Through the passing of time there will be united kingdoms and divided kingdoms. The Ark of My Presence will be in the hands of Israel and the hands of the enemy. There will be prophets who weep over My words and prophets who become bitter because of My mercy. People will grow, people will die, and at a certain point I will go silent for hundreds of years, saying nothing. Abraham, will you say yes?"

Abraham: "What? You want me to say yes to You? Did you hear all the bad things that would happen if I say yes? Sure, there are some good things that will happen, but there is so much more bad that will occur. How can I say yes to the bad, and then You determine to just go silent?"

God: "Hold on, Abraham, it gets better. Just because man is not hearing me doesn't mean that I am not at hand, working on behalf of man. They will be unable to see that I am waiting for a young lady named Mary. I will cause My Spirit to come upon her and she will become pregnant with My Son, Immanuel. During the pregnancy of Mary, she will also have a cousin who will be pregnant late in her life with John the Baptist. John will be a voice crying in the wilderness, prophesying about the coming of the Lamb of God. There will be a day that Jesus will come to John at the Jordan River to be baptized. From there I will declare that this is My Son. Jesus will go to the wilderness to be tempted by Satan, but He will also come out with power. The life of My Son will be marked by signs, wonders, and miracles. Abraham, Jesus will raise the dead, heal the blind, open deaf ears, heal lepers, cast out demons, walk on water, multiply loaves and fish to feed a multitude, and much more. However, the religious leaders will hate Him, and they will eventually capture Him to have Him beaten, His flesh will be ripped from His body, His beard will be plucked from His face. They will put a crown of thorns on His head, drive nails into His hands and feet, and as they mock Him they will have Him crucified on a cross. Abraham, will you say yes?"

Abraham: "How could You expect me to say yes to that? Did You not hear what they will do to Your Son?"

God: "But Abraham, that doesn't mean it's over. It gets better. They will place His body in a borrowed tomb and there will come a time when you, Abraham, will be in Paradise. There you will be with Jeremiah, Isaiah, David, and so many others. Maybe in the moment David will look up to see someone coming toward you all with a set of keys. David may exclaim, 'Look, it's the one who was crucified in the midst of the bulls of Bashan.' Then maybe Isaiah runs up to declare, 'Father Abraham, behold the lamb who was pierced for our transgressions.' Jeremiah might declare, 'Father Abraham, it's Him, it's the one I saw coming to set the captives free.' Abraham, don't you get it? Your *yes* is more than just about you. Your yes is about everyone who is affected by your yes. Abraham, will you say yes?"

Abraham: "Yes, Lord, I say *yes!*"

Sadly, this did not happen and this whole conversation has been nothing more than a figment of my imagination. Though we want the Lord to lay everything before us so that we can determine if the cost is too much to endure or not, it just doesn't happen that way. That's not faith, and that's not how all of the prophetic promises of your life are going to happen.

YOUR YES

But imagine for one moment that the Lord told you to leave everything you've known and everyone you have a relationship with (except your spouse) behind and go to place that He hasn't revealed to you yet, but you'll learn the location sometime along the journey. Many right now would be saying, "Yeah right!"

We are so convinced that the Lord would never ask us to be this bold in a blind faith, and yet this is exactly what the Lord required of Abraham. Honestly, we have a tendency to read the Word of God and admire the men and women but sincerely believe that the Lord would never ask of us the things that He asked so many in "Bible times." We are convinced that our purpose is to "get saved" and tarry until the Lord comes, or be ready to die and dodge hell so that we won't know eternal punishment. We rarely consider what God is requiring us to do, which will call upon great faith in the depths of who you are. The truth is, there could be challenges in our own lives that are similar to Abraham's. The question is, are you willing to say yes?

> *In hope against hope he believed, so that he might become a father of many nations according to that which had been spoken, "So shall your descendants be." Without becoming weak in faith he contemplated his own body, now as good as dead since he was about a hundred years old, and the deadness of Sarah's womb; yet, with respect to the promise of God, he did not waver in unbelief but grew strong in faith, giving glory to God, and being fully assured that what God had promised, He was able also to perform* (Romans 4:18-21).

Abraham's faith in the Lord was driven by the fact that he was hearing the Lord. That kind of relationship is what made him so strong in faith. I want to encourage you to understand the value of cultivating your relationship with the Lord. Don't allow a Sunday morning service to be the definition of that relationship. Spend time in His Word, in prayer, and in worship. Don't be the person who only experiences weekend visitation. Your faith must be a deep conviction born from the relationship that you have with God. When you cultivate that relationship, you will soon be reminded and encouraged that God's words are true. Because His words are true, we also know that God will perform all that He promises. Abraham simply believed that God was going to do what He said. We all know it and often declare that nothing is too hard or impossible for God. It's the step between knowing and activating that hinders our walk with the prophetic promises of God.

We know these things, but we all still find ourselves struggling with the implications of faith in our lives. God gives us a dream, but that dream is something that could potentially happen late in our lives. We have a vision, but in that vision we are a lot older than we are in the moment of the vision. A man or woman of God speaks a prophetic word into our life, but the timeline is many years in advance. Why would the Lord show us something so far into our lives? Why only give us a glimpse of something with a high possibility that we may never live to see it?

It's interesting that we never consider what the Lord said to Abraham about his own destiny. God told Abraham that generations would come from him, so many that the descendants would outnumber the sands of the shores and the stars of the sky. Imagine hearing a prophetic word that speaks into your family's destiny but never seeing the fulfillment of that word. Now in our natural mind we may be quick to say that Abraham had to know that he would never live to see that unfold. And possibly that may be true, but like us all, Abraham could have had this desire to see it revealed in his own lifetime. So what made Abraham able to follow the Lord with this great faith?

THE TEST OF FAITH

Abraham was tested! None of us want to hear this because we don't like to be tested, but the truth is that God put Abraham through tests in order to see him advance. Though Abraham said yes, he would be tested. Many of us may be at the point in our lives where we are willing to be tested, and through those tests we understand that increase is coming. This is where we find a huge key in understanding how Abraham could have endured the test from the Lord, and what made his kind of faith possible for us when it comes to our prophetic promises.

> *By faith Abraham, when he was tested, offered up Isaac, and he who had received the promises was offering up his only begotten son; it was he to whom it was said, "In Isaac your descendants shall be called." He considered that God is able to raise people even from the dead, from which he also received him back as a type* (Hebrews 11:17-19).

By now I imagine that you have heard a message preached or a lesson from a teacher about how Abraham was prepared to take the life of his son, Isaac. We hear how Abraham knew that even if he had taken the life of his son, God was going to raise him from the dead. We quickly say amen but never stop to think about how he knew. Let's be honest with ourselves for a moment. If the Lord promised you a child and then told you to take his or her life, how confident would you be that God would raise that child from the dead? Many of us would say yes. Some may not even hesitate. And to you I say—awesome. To everyone else, I want to encourage you because God gives us these prophetic promises for a specific reason.

Here is where I want to challenge your faith. I want to challenge the fact that what you may be defining as faith is possibly not faith at all. Let me ask you:

- Do you have the faith to see someone get out of a wheelchair?

- Do you have the faith to see someone healed of cancer?

- Do you have the faith to see someone's back healed and straightened up?

- Do you have the faith to see someone's addictions broken?

- Do you have the faith to see blind eyes opened?

- Do you have the faith to see deaf ears opened?

- Do you have the faith to see the mute speak?

I imagine that everyone reading that list is going to respond with a resounding yes. Now I want to ask you:

- Have you seen someone get out of a wheelchair (in person, on a video, on a TV program, etc.)?

- Have you seen someone healed of cancer (in person, on a video, on a TV program, etc.)?

- Have you seen someone's back straightened up (in person, on a video, on a TV program, etc.)?

- Have you seen someone have their addictions broken (in person, on a video, on a TV program, etc.)?

- Have you seen blind eyes opened (in person, on a video, on a TV program, etc.)?

- Have you seen deaf ears opened (in person, on a video, on a TV program, etc.)?

- Have you seed someone who couldn't speak all of sudden speak (in person, on a video, on a TV program, etc.)?

Chances are, you have seen or been a part of the above examples. When we have seen these things it immediately encourages us to believe for more. Unfortunately, we now have predetermined our faith based off of what we have seen. When we see someone get up from a wheelchair, we declare that we have the faith to believe for others to be healed. Now our faith is no longer based off of things not yet seen; rather, we are determining the measure of our faith off of what we have seen.

Many of us have inadvertently set our faith by the standard of what we have witnessed, but that isn't faith. It's not like Abraham could have said, "I believe that if I take the life of my son, the Lord is going to raise him from the dead because He did for George when George took the life of his son." When God told Abraham to kill his son, a resurrected life had never been done before. Before you get all spiritual on me and remind me that God promised Abraham all these descendants through Isaac, let me ask you—how confident would you have been if you were in the place of Abraham? Let's face it, we would have been struggling to be obedient and take the life of Isaac.

This is where we find a secret unfolding for us. In Hebrews 11:19, it tells us that Abraham had *considered* that God could raise someone from the dead. Abraham *considered* it. Hmm, that is an interesting word to describe what Abraham was processing. Does it mean that Abraham simply sat down for a while and began to think about things? Did he run things over and over through his mind, ultimately coming to the conclusion that if he killed Isaac, God would raise him from the dead?

That word "considered" comes from the Greek word *logizomai* (Strong's #G3049), which is rooted in another Greek word—*logos* (Strong's #G3056). The Greek word *logos* is where we get the written Word of God. You have the written Word (*logos*) and the spoken word (*rhema*). At this moment in time Abraham, did not have the written Word of the Lord. It's not like Abraham could make a trip to the local shopping center and purchase a Bible for himself to reference what God had said. In the time of Abraham, the word of the Lord would be transcribed on staffs and those staffs would be passed on through generations. *Logos* is where we get the Latin word *logicae*, which ultimately gave us the English word *logic*. Logic is the polar opposite of faith. Logic is faith's greatest nemesis as faith deals with what we cannot yet see, while logic deals with common sense. You know those moments where the Lord is calling you to step out in faith, but then there is an overload of people reminding you to have common sense about what you are doing. It's funny how we do our best to implement common sense into the realm of faith. Yet, throughout the Bible we can see a multitude of experiences where God moved in ways that rarely made sense, and most definitely wasn't common.

So what happened? Did Abraham just sit and think about it? Did he simply consider the options of death and life? Did he get to the point where it just made sense to take the life of his son (the promise). After all it's just common sense to kill the prophetic promise of your life.

CHAPTER 4

THE CHALLENGES WE FACE

"I believe you are destined to do great things. God created you for a purpose. He has opportunities He wants to give you and assignments with which He wants to entrust you."
—JOYCE MEYER, *Never Give Up!*

I n living our lives, we face difficulties and challenges that can often be overwhelming. Whether it is something that involves our employment, our marriage, our children, our family, and/or our friends, no life is lived without trials or tribulations. We face challenges that will either break us or makes us better than we were before. It's never an easy part of life, but it is a part of all of our lives. What may appear to be too big of a challenge for one person may be a minor one for another. We can't get into the habit of comparing our lives with others. Although we model our "Christianity" on many in the Bible, we seldom embrace those challenges with a brave face. Many will profess to love the Lord with all of their heart, and then the very moment that it becomes difficult they vanish back into the world.

No one likes to be tested. Even if God came and stood before you to tell you that you were about to be tested, but don't fear you will come through this fire—more than likely you wouldn't be eagerly signing up. Even those who have strong lives of faith will find themselves struggling to follow through at times. We tell ourselves that God will never put more on us than we are willing to endure. Funny how that works. We misquote scripture to help us wink at our failures of obedience. The problem is that God will allow more to come upon us than we are willing to endure. The actual scripture reads:

> *No temptation has overtaken you but such as is common to man; and God is faithful, who will not allow you to be tempted beyond what you are able, but with the temptation will provide the way of escape also, so that you will be able to endure it* (1 Corinthians 10:13).

The verse is actually saying that God *"will not allow you to be tempted beyond what you are able."* This means that when the challenges of our lives become more than what we can handle, we must learn to cry out to the Lord. If you could handle it alone, without God helping you, then you would never call upon the Lord. When it is more than we can endure, we have an Abba Father we can call upon and He will provide for us what we need in the challenge.

Abraham was faced with a serious challenge. We could even say it was a dilemma for his life. In Genesis 12:1-3, the Lord gave Abraham a prophetic word over his life.

> *Now the Lord said to Abram, "Go forth from your country, and from your relatives and from your father's house, to the land which I will show you; and I will make you a great nation, and I will bless you, and make your name great; and so you shall be a blessing; and I will bless those who bless you, and the one who curses you I will curse. And in you all the families of the earth will be blessed."*

Actually, it would be the beginning of another prophetic word spoken into his life. In Genesis 15 we find the story of the Lord coming to Abram in a vision. The Lord told Abram that He would be a shield to him and Abram's reward would be great. Abram began to converse with the Lord, asking what reward would come to him. At the time Abram had no children or heir. It's one of the most quoted moments in the life of anyone in the Bible. The Lord told Abram to look to the heavens and see the number of stars. An heir would come from him, and through that heir he would have as many descendants as there were stars. Can you imagine the impact of receiving this kind of word from the Lord? But it gets so much better.

The Lord told Abram that He was the one who brought him out of Ur of the Chaldeans, to give him the land in order to possess it. Abram questions the Lord, as many of us would do. He immediately asks the Lord how he (Abram) was going to possess the land. At this point the scripture in Genesis 15 describes Abram as having already begun to believe in the Lord. We could say that his faith was being activated. The Lord then called upon Abram to bring Him a three-year-old heifer, a three-year-old female goat, a three-year-old ram, a turtledove, and a pigeon. After Abram prepared the animals for a sacrifice he fell into a deep sleep. While asleep, the Lord revealed to Abram that his descendants would be strangers in a land that was not theirs. In that land they would become slaves for four hundred years.

Now this would be the point where many of us would be checking out on the prophecy about our life and the lives of our descendants. This doesn't appear to be a very encouraging word. However, the Lord wasn't done speaking to Abram. The Lord then told Abram that He would judge the nation where they would serve as slaves, and there would be a time that they would come out of bondage with many possessions. The Lord finished what He was speaking into Abram by allowing him to know that he would live to be an old man. On that day, the Lord made a covenant with Abram.

Get this understanding—Abram was promised a son. Not only a son, but descendants too many to number. What a prophetic word to personally receive from the Lord. Granted, there were parts in there that I imagine Abram did not want to hear or receive, but just imagine what was going through his mind. Especially when the time came in Abram's life to see the fulfillment of that word. The faith of Abram is better understood with the birth of his son, Isaac.

Abram and Sarai had no children of their own, which would have been considered shameful in the culture of their day. Then the Lord promised through a prophetic vision that Abram would have a son. Isaac would be the heir of Abram's life, the fulfillment of promise. Then, God reinforced His promise to Abram in Genesis 17 as the Lord intervened in the life of Abram and Sarai. At this point in his life, Abram was 99 years old. The Lord appeared to Abram with a declaration and reminder of the covenant that they had with each other. The Lord declared to Abram that he would now be called Abraham. The Lord was making Abraham the father of a multitude of nations. Abraham would be exceedingly fruitful, and from Abraham there would come forth nations. There would even be kings in the lineage of Abraham. The Lord would extend His covenant with Abraham to his descendants and throughout their generations for an everlasting covenant with the Lord. The beauty of this word came when the Lord also said to Abraham that He would be their God. Such a powerful word—and the Lord wasn't done yet! Then God said to Abraham that his wife, Sarai, would also be renamed, and He would bless her and give Abraham a son by her. Sarah would become a mother of nations, and kings of peoples would come from her.

You would think many of us, at this point, would get excited about such a word coming into our lives. But that wasn't the case with Abraham, and it's often not the case with us when we receive words from the Lord. When Abraham heard the word about a son, he fell on his face and laughed, asking the Lord if a child could be born to a man one hundred years old. Not only that, but Sarah was ninety years old. Here in this chapter we discover that Ishmael was already conceived from Abraham and Hagar, the servant of Sarah. It's why Abraham tried to insert Ishmael into the fulfillment of this prophetic promise.

Abraham did what we often do. He tried to use a now moment to explain a future time so that little to no faith would be required for something that could not yet be tangibly seen. The problem for Abraham was that the promise was for him and Sarah. The covenant would be for Isaac. Keep in mind that Abraham was 99 years old when he fully received the prophetic promise of the Lord and carried out the commands through the circumcision of his flesh.

Abraham didn't always do everything right in his life. He made mistakes and poor decisions. Having a child with Hagar would definitely be an example of a poor decision and not thinking things through. Humankind has always had a way of rushing the process of the Lord when we feel like He is taking too long. You may have heard the saying, "The Lord is an on-time God. He is never early or late." We say that, but seldom do we actually believe that the Lord is on time. If we are honest, we feel like He misses a lot of great opportunities to be on (our) time.

Let's think about the very moment that the Lord told Abraham to leave his country and everyone behind except for his wife. Yet it's interesting that Abraham did not do that. Oh, he left, and he took Sarah, but he also took his nephew, Lot. This ended up causing a lot of hardship between two camps that caused a separation and a time when Abraham did his best to intervene on behalf of Lot's life. The truth is, Lot should have never been there to begin with, but the Lord permitted him to go. Things like this should comfort us that even the great heroes of faith made poor decisions and mistakes along the way. No one is perfect, and we aren't always going to get it 100 percent right. However, we must be determined to live a life where we *"walk by faith, not by sight"* (2 Cor. 5:7).

So how did Abraham become this great father of faith? Why does Hebrews specifically mention the time in Abraham's life when the Lord tested him with the life of Isaac? I'm glad you asked!

PASSING THE TEST

When we study Genesis 22, we need to remind ourselves of some very important aspects concerning the life and example of Abraham. Now, we don't like to admit it, but the Lord will test us. When we are going through something very difficult or challenging it is often easier to blame the enemy and call it an attack on our life, rather than acknowledge that it is a test from the Lord. The very beginning of Genesis 22 clearly states that the Lord tested Abraham. I know, I know. The idea of the Lord testing us is such hard pill to swallow, but it is a biblical truth that God will grow and mature us in our faith. There are three key verses that I want to highlight here.

> *Now it came about after these things, that God tested Abraham, and said to him, "Abraham!" And he said, "Here I am." He said, "Take now your son, your only son, whom you love, Isaac, and go to the land of Moriah, and offer him there as a burnt offering on one of the mountains of which I will tell you." So Abraham rose early in the morning and saddled his donkey, and took two of his young men with him and Isaac his son; and he split wood for the burnt offering, and arose and went to the place of which God had told him. On the third day Abraham raised his eyes and saw the place from a distance* (Genesis 22:1-4).

Shortly thereafter, Abraham told the men who came with him and Isaac that they were going to a certain location where they would worship and return. As they began their process, Abraham took the wood for the offering and laid it on Isaac. Abraham and Isaac walked on together. Isaac asked his father where the offering was. They had the wood, the fire, and the knife, but there was no animal. Abraham responded by saying that God would provide a lamb for the burnt offering. Can you imagine what is possibly running through the minds of Abraham and Isaac? From Isaac's point of view, nothing made any sense because of the missing offering. From the view of Abraham, was he questioning within himself? Had he truly believed in the Lord? Was his faith strong enough to go through with the command from the Lord? Would the Lord provide? As they came to the place of which God had told Abraham, he built the altar there. Arranging the wood and preparing the fire, Abraham bound Isaac on the altar.

If you can, imagine Isaac stretched across the altar and the moment Abraham stretched out his hand, taking the knife to kill his son. We could never imagine the difficulty of this moment, but we do understand that Abraham was fully committed. So committed that the angel of the Lord had to call out Abraham's name twice. After Abraham responded, the angel told him not to strike Isaac with the knife. The angel also told Abraham that because of his obedience and because he did not withhold his son from the Lord, God now knew that Abraham feared Him. What a test! But remember earlier when Isaac asked his father about a sacrifice and Abraham responded that the Lord would provide.

Then Abraham raised his eyes and looked, and behold, behind him a ram caught in the thicket by his horns; and Abraham went and took the

*ram and offered him up for a burnt offering in
the place of his son* (Genesis 22:13).

The Lord will provide! After Abraham took the ram
for an offering, the angel of the Lord called to Abraham
a second time and began detailing that through his son,
Isaac, Abraham would be blessed and his seed would be
multiplied as the stars of the heavens and as the sand
which is on the seashore. If that isn't enough to get
someone excited, the angel then added that the seed of
Abraham would possess the gates of their enemies, and
all the nations of the earth would be blessed because
Abraham obeyed the Lord.

We have a tendency to read these scriptures and our
level of respect and admiration for Abraham goes way up
high. How could a father ever get to the point of taking
the life of his only son (through Sarah) and have an angel
of the Lord call out his name twice because he was so
committed? Think about how many messages you have
heard about the faith of Abraham. In each of those messages how many times did they tell us that Abraham
knew that the Lord would raise him from the dead? I ask
this because I want to know if it was that simple? Was
it just the fact that by this time in the life of Abraham
he had total trust in the Lord, and no matter what the
test may be, Abraham was going to be determined faithful? Did Abraham just know that the Lord would never

permit the life of Isaac to never breath again? What if I told you that his challenge wasn't in taking the life of his son, but the challenge was trusting in what the Lord had promised?

Look again closely at Genesis 22:1. I know that none of us want to be tested, but it's abundantly clear that the Lord is testing Abraham. With that in mind, get how Abraham responded, "Here I am." I never thought anything about that statement until I had an English professor come to me one night after a service and said, "You know, Ryan, that's not proper English." Honestly, I mentally rolled my eyes because I could not care less at that time about the English language. And then she said, "Ryan, proper English would have said, 'Here am I.'" In my mind I thought, *Well, la-dee-freaking-da*. But it hit me! By this time in Abraham's life he had spent enough time with the Lord that his vocabulary had changed. Abraham was speaking like the Lord. This is so important for you and me. We have got to be people who spend time with the Father.

WHAT ABRAHAM SAW

Look closely at Genesis 22:2. The Lord told Abraham to take his only son and sacrifice him on one of the mountains that the Lord would tell him. This particular place was in the land of Moriah. That's so important!

Look closely at Genesis 22:3. Abraham woke up to prepare everything for the moment of the sacrifice and went to the place God told him to go. Do you see that? In verse 2, "I'll tell you where to go," and in verse 3 Abraham went where God told him to go.

Look closely at Genesis 22:4. Abraham saw a place from a distance. What place? If verse 3 tells us that Abraham is going to the place God told him, what place did he see from that distance?

There are clues throughout scripture here. First of all, let's look at the fact that Abraham is in the land of Moriah. You can visit the land of Moriah to this day. If you were to do an internet search on Jerusalem, you would see the land of Moriah. More than likely the first thing you would see is a gold dome with the old walls from the City of David below it. Yep, the land of Moriah is the region we see today as the city of Jerusalem. It's important to know this because it would be the same place where Jesus would be crucified outside of the city walls of Jerusalem. Jesus was crucified in the land of Moriah at Golgotha. The very place where the Lord had directed Abraham to sacrifice his only son Isaac, God would one day have His own Son sacrificed there many years later. Oh, it gets better.

There is a key word in verse 4 when it says that *"Abraham raised his eyes and saw."* Why is this important?

In verse 13, *"Abraham raised his eyes and looked."* Two similar descriptions but two different words describing how Abraham viewed something. In verse 4 he *saw*. In verse 13 he *looked*. What could Abraham had *seen* from a distance, on a third day, in the land of Moriah? It was here that the Lord began to speak to me about how He gave a spiritual vision to Abraham of the death, burial, and resurrection of His own Son, Jesus. When Abraham looked, there was a literal ram caught in the thicket to replace his son Isaac. But the moment he saw the place from a distance on the third day in the place where Jesus would bear the cross, it was a vision to get Abraham to fulfill the test.

Okay, some of you are probably doubting that God would show Abraham the death, burial, and resurrection of Jesus just so that Abraham would go through with sacrificing his own son. I'm glad you doubted.

Your father Abraham rejoiced to see My day,
and he saw it and was glad (John 8:56).

Here in John 8, this is Jesus talking. He is detailing how Abraham saw His day and rejoiced. This is long before Jesus ever went to Jerusalem to be arrested in the garden. Long before Jesus would be beaten at the whipping post. Long before Jesus would carry the cross to Golgotha. Long before Jesus would have nails driven into His hands and feet. Long before Jesus would wear a crown a thorns. Long before the dead body of Jesus would be laid in a borrowed tomb. Long before Jesus would be resurrected and witnessed by the disciples and a multitude of others. Jesus declared that Abraham saw His day! The Lord gave Abraham a prophetic glimpse of His own Son's death and resurrection, thereby strengthening the faith of Abraham.

The challenge we face is not what we perceive it to be. Many have been given prophetic words over our lives, but those words have a great distance of time attached to them. It's not that God is showing us these things with some kind of lost hope that we may see them; rather, He is showing us for the purpose of fulfilling the promises. The challenge we face is when we are given a prophetic dream, a prophetic vision, and/or a prophetic word— will we embrace the end of the story so that we live out the rest?

CHAPTER 5

IS IT FAITH OR IS IT TRUST

*"Never be afraid to trust an unknown
future to a known God."*
—CORRIE TEN BOOM

There's a huge difference between trusting in our own works and trusting in God. We would agree that there is a difference between depending upon the law to redeem us versus living a life of faith in the finished work of the cross. Obviously, faith is developed in our lives as we do good works.

But are you willing to recognize, you foolish fellow, that faith without works is useless? Was not Abraham our father justified by works when he offered up Isaac his son on the altar? You see that faith was working with his works, and as a result of the works, faith was perfected; and the Scripture was fulfilled which says, "And Abraham believed God, and it was reckoned to him as righteousness," and he was called the friend of God. You see that a man is justified by works and not by faith alone (James 2:20-24).

We should have the heart to desire to do good works through our faith. Abraham believed in the truth from the Lord. Abraham also demonstrated this faith through the messengers of the Lord as well.

But is it that simple? Do we have to consistently stay determined to connect our faith to the promises of the Lord? Or is it a trust issue that hinders our ability to have the kind of faith that we need to see the Lord move on our behalf? By now, most of us will easily determine that our faith is either strong or weak. Will we be pleased with our answer? Let's go back to the understanding that we gained from the father in Mark 9:24: *"Immediately the boy's father cried out and said, 'I do believe; help my unbelief.'"*

For the majority of us, our faith does have a weakening that is easily hidden. One of the most difficult aspects of faith is our ability to trust in the Lord. We all say that we do, but in hindsight we fail to connect our faith with trust. Truthfully, it's so much easier to say that we have faith for something and feel good about that level of faith. It's in those moments of being tested that we are marked by unbelief. We unwillingly agree with the mindset of not trusting while professing that we believe. It's not easy, and I do not mean to imply that it is. I am stating these things to bring revelation and recognition to where we lose our battles for our prophetic promises.

WHO WE SAY HE IS

In Matthew 16 we see the story of Jesus sitting down with the disciples in Caesarea Philippi. There Jesus would ask His disciples, *"Who do people say that the Son of Man is?"* The disciples respond by saying, *"Some say John the Baptist; and others, Elijah; but still others, Jeremiah, or one of the prophets"* (Matt. 16:13-14). What fascinates me is the fact that Jesus then asked the same question, but in a different manner. *"But who do you say that I am?"* Simon Barjona speaks up to respond, *"You are the Christ, the Son of the living God"* (Matt. 16:15-16). Immediately Jesus said:

> *Blessed are you, Simon Barjona, because flesh and blood did not reveal this to you, but My Father who is in heaven. I also say to you that you are Peter, and upon this rock I will build*

*My church; and the gates of Hades will not over-
power it. I will give you the keys of the kingdom
of heaven; and whatever you bind on earth shall
have been bound in heaven, and whatever you
loose on earth shall have been loosed in heaven*
(Matthew 16:17-19).

What a powerful revelation and word spoken to
Simon Peter. Now, before he or the other disciples could
process what had just occurred, Jesus warned them that
they could not tell anyone that He was the Christ. Once
again, Jesus began to go into detail of what was coming.
He began to share that He had to go to Jerusalem where
he would end up suffering many things from the elders,
chief priests, and scribes. He shared with the disciples
that there in Jerusalem He would be killed, but He would
also be raised from the dead on the third day. Although
Simon Peter had received this revelation from the Father
that Jesus was the Christ, the news of His suffering and
death was more than he could handle. Simon Peter took
Jesus aside and actually began to rebuke Jesus. That's bold
right there! Simon Peter told Jesus that it would never
happen, as if Peter wasn't only rebuking Jesus for speaking this way but also telling Jesus that Simon Peter would
never allow it to happen. What happens next is a surprise
to us all as Jesus declared, *"Get behind Me, Satan! You are
a stumbling block to Me; for you are not setting your mind
on God's interests, but man's"* (Matt. 16:23).

Jesus had the disciples at the place of revelation. They answered Jesus according to what others were saying. Jesus then asked the same question in a different word structure and got a response from Simon Barjona (Peter). Simon's response was remarkable because it revealed that no one had told him this but the Father in heaven. That moment of personal revelation of who Jesus truly was also opened the revelation of who Simon was. Like Simon Barjona, we too find ourselves unable to know who we really are without first having the revelation of who Jesus is. When Simon Barjona knew Jesus as the Christ, he got a revelation that he was no longer Simon Barjona, but he would be Peter (*Petra*—rock). With that revelation came the purpose of the Ekklesia (the church—legislative governing authority).

Let's remind ourselves of a few things. In verse 21 we see that Jesus began telling the disciples about His destiny in Jerusalem. By this time, it would have been a lot easier to have faith and believe in what Jesus was telling the disciples. By this moment in time the disciples had witnessed healings, miracles, walking on water, causing storms to cease, physical objects multiplying, the dead raised, and much more. It would seem that when Jesus said that He was going to die but be raised up on the third day, this wouldn't be that difficult to have faith in. Right?

Let's go back to verse 22 where Peter took Jesus to the side and rebuked Jesus. Whoa! Who has the audacity to rebuke the Son of God? Simon Barjona, a.k.a. Peter. Yep, Peter rebuked Jesus, saying that he would never allow this to happen to Jesus. Jesus then responded with a rebuke of His own. With that rebuke He identified Peter as a stumbling block. Jesus told Peter that he wasn't setting his mind on God's interests but his own (or the interests of humankind). This is fascinating to me. I do not believe it was a faith issue for Peter or the disciples. Rather, it was a trust issue. Granted, we don't have an exact scripture highlighting this, but we can get an idea of how trust could have been a major hindrance.

Peter could have not fully trusted Jesus in His decision to go to Jerusalem, or he could have not trusted those who would be around Jesus during the time. Regardless of whether it was in Jesus or in other individuals, there appears to be a lack of trust. Many times, we are just like Peter. We hear the declarations that others make when the Lord has given them a destiny or a purpose. We want to have faith in them, and some days we do, but truthfully when we see the person or those around them, we find ourselves challenged to trust them in the process. We all know that we need to believe that God can do the impossible in our lives. We all know that nothing is too difficult for the Lord. We all need to get to the place where we believe in the power and promises of the Lord. In all of our efforts to believe (have faith), we also recognize the importance of being obedient to God. Sometimes we have this mastered, and other days maybe not so much. Along with that belief, that faith, we also need to trust the Lord's guidance.

We have to learn to trust Him with the direction He is leading us. We need to look into the depth of our faith and learn how to trust the Lord with every bit of our being. The prophetic dreams, visions, and words over our future should motivate us to live by faith while trusting the Lord to fulfill His promises whether we see it or not.

> *Oh, the depth of the riches both of the wisdom and knowledge of God! How unsearchable are His judgments and unfathomable His ways! For who has known the mind of the Lord, or who became His counselor? Or who has first given to Him that it might be paid back to him again? For from Him and through Him and to Him are all things. To Him be the glory forever. Amen* (Romans 11:33-36).

Trusting in the promises of the Lord with complete, unadulterated faith can be extremely tough. We have to consciously lay aside our own agendas and precon- ceived expectations. Though we know this, we must be reminded to surrender to the plans of the Lord.

STUMBLING BLOCKS

What if we don't feel like we can trust the Lord with certain aspects of our lives? I know, one might ask, "How could we ever not trust the Lord?"

For many individuals, their concept of the Lord is based on the kind of relationship that they had with someone who was influential in their life. For example, some individuals develop a view of God based on the kind of relationship they had with their father. If that relationship was tense and always had them walking around on pins and needles, over time they could develop a mentality that God is about to lose His cool at any moment if they do something to upset Him. With some, they may have never had a father in their life, and with that abandonment they can develop the mindset that God isn't ever there when it matters most.

With some it's parental; with others it's with bosses or leaders in the church. Humankind has the tendency to develop an idea of who God is based off of our own experiences with others. Whether those experiences were good or bad, it can sway our understanding of the Lord. This is ultimately why Jesus first asked the disciples, "Who do they say I am?" Jesus was asking the disciples how they viewed Him based off of what others were saying about Him. That's why it's so important that He asked Simon Barjona specifically who he (Peter) said He was.

When you have a skewed view of the Lord, it can hinder your ability to trust Him. It's the same with how we treat those around us. If someone gives you insight into someone's life whom you have never met in person, you will develop a mindset of how you will receive them or reject them based solely off of the words of others. It happens every single day.

> *Do not love the world nor the things in the world. If anyone loves the world, the love of the Father is not in him. For all that is in the world, the lust of the flesh and the lust of the eyes and the boastful pride of life, is not from the Father, but is from the world. The world is passing away, and also its lusts; but the one who does the will of God lives forever* (1 John 2:15-17).

There is a daily battle in our lives because we live in the world, but we most definitely are not of this world (if you are born again). It's because of this world that we find it so difficult to trust the Lord. However, we can be encouraged through the Word of the Lord. Jesus would say to the disciples and to us today:

> *If the world hates you, you know that it has hated Me before it hated you. If you were of the*

world, the world would love its own; but because you are not of the world, but I chose you out of the world, because of this the world hates you (John 15:18-19).

Later, Jesus would be spending time with the Father, and through that prayer we understand that Jesus covered with prayer the disciples and those who would become disciples in the future.

I have given them Your word; and the world has hated them, because they are not of the world, even as I am not of the world. I do not ask You to take them out of the world, but to keep them from the evil one. They are not of the world, even as I am not of the world. Sanctify them in the truth; Your word is truth. As You sent Me into the world, I also have sent them into the world. For their sakes I sanctify Myself, that they themselves also may be sanctified in truth (John 17:14-19).

John the Beloved reminds us to make sure that our hearts are devoted to the Father above anything in the world that could hinder our relationship with the Lord.

Don't set the affections of your heart on this world or in loving the things of the world. The love of the Father and the love of the world are incompatible (1 John 2:15 TPT).

When Paul sent his letter to the Romans, he had to address the lure of becoming like the culture around them. Instead of turning their hearts and minds to the Lord, they could easily be swayed by the opinions of others.

Stop imitating the ideals and opinions of the culture around you, but be inwardly transformed by the Holy Spirit through a total reformation of how you think. This will empower you to discern God's will as you live a beautiful life, satisfying and perfect in his eyes (Romans 12:2 TPT).

When we lack trust, we become stumbling blocks to the fulfillment of those dreams, visions, and words. Time and time again I have heard the stories of people who have given up on the Lord. They become angry and bitter toward God. They had a dream, a vision, or a word from a man or woman of God, but with the passing of time they failed to see any evidence that those prophetic promises had any hope. I can't tell you how many times I have heard from an angry parent who was promised that their child would come to know the Lord. In each of those cases, a lot of time had passed, and with each year slipping away that child seemed further and further away from the Lord. They become bitter at the people who gave them hope. They get mad at the church. They declare certain individuals are false prophets, and sadly many will soon wage war against the Body of Christ. It's so easy to put ourselves above everything else in this world. Especially when we have those dreams, visions, and words. We immediately have hope, we walk in faith, and we declare our trust. It's funny how when something good happens we are quick to congratulate ourselves on having faith. Yet when something bad happens, we find someone or something to blame so that we can feel better about it not happening the way that we intended it to.

When it comes to prophetic promises, it is neither a faith issue nor a trust issue alone. Rather, it's the co-laboring of faith and trust going hand in hand. When the Lord gives us a promise, we must learn to have faith in what He is saying. Equally important is our ability to trust the Lord enough to recognize that if He said it, He will fulfill it. If we have the faith that He can, we must trust that He will. It's time to be honest with ourselves. We will find every excuse in the book when it comes to explaining away our behavior, our decisions, and the sins we cover up.

The heart is more deceitful than all else and is desperately sick; who can understand it? (Jeremiah 17:9)

IN HIS HANDS

We have to get to the point in our lives where we see how much we truly need the Lord to move on our behalf. We know that when we receive these prophetic promises, there is an activation that must come from us. The problem is that we can easily begin to think that we can control certain aspects of our lives, therefore directing the fulfillment of the promises.

Again, think back to what Jesus told Peter when He said that Peter was not thinking with the mind of God but for the interests of man. This happens so often in our lives. When we have these dreams, visions, or words, we can put our faith in the Lord yet our trust in ourselves or others. This is why we have to remember that the heart is deceitful. We don't want to hear it, but the truth is that the moment we get a glimpse of what we have longed for, we will do what we can to get it done without ever considering the effect on others. There is a timing with all prophetic promises that we fail to understand or cooperate with. Had Peter been able to hinder the destiny of Jesus, the timing would have been affected in ways he may never have considered. And yet the Bible states that Jesus was slain before the foundation of the earth (see Rev. 13:8 NKJV). Long before Jesus would be crucified, destiny was attached to it.

Your prophetic promises are before you, and the destinies of many have yet to be fulfilled. With that in mind I want to encourage you to continue to walk daily with faith and never stop trusting the Lord. God has shown you a glimpse for a purpose. Now trust the process, because you know that the Lord cannot lie!

> *And those who know Your name will put their trust in You; for You, Lord, have not forsaken those who seek You* (Psalm 9:10 NKJV).

CHAPTER 6

THE BLUEPRINT OF FAITH

"Whatever God has called you to do, He has also gifted you to do it. You may not have heeded God's call on your life in the past, but that call is still there. The gifts and callings of God are without repentance! Make a decision today to stir up the gift within you and to fulfill the call of God."
—KENNETH E. HAGIN,
The Gifts and Calling of God

WHAT IS HOPE?

Now faith is the substance of things hoped for, the evidence of things not seen (Hebrews 11:1 NKJV).

Let's go back and look at how our faith is built. When we are getting a better understanding of how we must apply faith to our prophetic promises, we need to see clearly how that structure is maintained. It's not really about having some great admiration for these men and women we read about in Hebrews 11; it's actually having the recognition that time may pass before the fulfillment of our dreams, visions, and words. We need to learn how to see the end of the story to encourage us to live out the rest of the story. "Substance of things *hoped* for"—what does this actually mean? What does our hope look like? What does our hope sound like? What exactly is hope?

According to *Vine's Expository Dictionary*, hope is defined as "favorable and confident expectation." The truth is, it has to do with the unseen and the future. But how do we know this? We have to go back and look at what Paul said.

> *For we were saved in this hope, but hope that is seen is not hope; for why does one still hope for what he sees? But if we hope for what we do not see, we eagerly wait for it with perseverance* (Romans 8:24-25 NKJV).

"Hope" is described as the anticipation of good.

> *In the hope of eternal life, which God, who cannot lie, promised long ages ago* (Titus 1:2).

Who through Him are believers in God, who raised Him from the dead and gave Him glory, so that your faith and hope are in God (1 Peter 1:21).

The foundation upon which "hope" is based is the glory of the Lord.

But when her masters saw that their hope of profit was gone, they seized Paul and Silas and dragged them into the market place before the authorities (Acts 16:19).

To whom God willed to make known what is the riches of the glory of this mystery among the Gentiles, which is Christ in you, the hope of glory (Colossians 1:27).

We soon learn to have our "hope" fixed or strengthened to be firm in Christ. In other words, not wavering but strong.

Paul, an apostle of Christ Jesus according to the commandment of God our Savior, and of Christ Jesus, who is our hope (1 Timothy 1:1).

Many won't have an issue with hope. We have learned how to hope for things in our lifetime. We hope for good days over the bad. We hope to see the Lord work on our behalf. We hope to have a peaceful life with a loving spouse and amazing children. We have hope in our dreams, our desires, our goals. Hope brings the fullness of our imagination into reality through the principle of faith. Although hope remains invisible to us at times, when it is connected with faith it opens us up to the potential of the impossible becoming possible.

Hope when cultivated with prayer forms the substance of our faith. Hope lays the foundation of the promises from the Lord. It's that substance we need to develop our confidence of our hope. The word for substance, *hupostasis,* actually means support, assurance, confidence (Strong's #G5287). When we pray, our expectations begin to increase because of the hope that we have through the faith in His promises. I would love to admit that many of us pray and never expect anything in return from the Lord, but the truth is that the majority of individuals rarely pray except at the moment of needing God to move on their behalf. We all need to be reminded that prayer cultivates the relationship that we have with the Lord, but if our relationship is one-sided and we only communicate with God because we need something, our view of faith will be limited to whether or not we actually see it now.

Have you ever noticed that when you read the promises of God throughout the scriptures, you quickly begin to envision exactly what you are reading? Then you begin to place yourself in those promises, and before you notice it hope is rising within your heart and affecting your mind. When we hear the testimonies, whether in the Word of God or in real life, they will immediately begin to stir you and increase your faith for certain things. Think about the first time you heard about Bartimaeus and how that put a charge in your spirit to believe that God could heal blind eyes. Or maybe the moment you read about the demon-possessed man being set free from his tormentors (demonic spirits), and with that you immediately thought about how so many lives could be changed by the power of Jesus.

Whether it came in the form of a story written in the Word of God or a real-life moment, these testimonies help to build our faith because they gave us the substance of hope. God permits these great testimonies to encourage us. They build the foundation of our hope. When we are in despair and feeling as though there is no hope, we see these testimonies unfold before us and suddenly we are overwhelmed with an increase.

This is probably the place where you are recalling what you read in Chapter 4 when I broke down how we view our faith. How we often define our faith on the ability to see things first. It's important to bring our attention to this because I want to make it clear that God is not saying that we cannot be encouraged by testimonies. In no way am I implying that God will not move on our behalf if we are encouraged by the testimonies that we read in the Word or the testimonies we have experienced or seen in life. Those testimonies play a vital role in our life. The truth is, we all have weak moments and find ourselves in difficult situations where we need encouragement. We need examples of how God has worked or how God has moved beyond the impossible circumstances. The point is that we cannot simply determine our faith by those testimonies themselves. We can't get to the point where we can only have the faith in what we have seen. There will be tests in our lives that we won't have any form of testimony to go by. Again, remember that when Abraham was going to sacrifice the life of his son Isaac, he didn't have any kind of testimony. And yet, the Lord encouraged Abraham by showing him a place from a great distance. We cultivate our prophetic promises with the testimonies of others and the Word, but we also learn how to have the faith to see what has yet to be seen.

The evidence of things *not yet* seen—how can there be evidence of things not seen? No one is ever convicted in a courtroom with evidence that cannot be seen, and yet it seems that God wants us to build from that very evidence. According to *Webster's Dictionary, evidence* means "an outward sign, something that furnishes proof, testimony, something legally submitted to a tribunal to ascertain the truth of a matter, or one who bears witness."

If I were to hand you a blueprint to build a house but that blueprint was lacking any measurements, you would find yourself challenged. That is often how people describe the fulfillment of prophetic promises in their lives. We have the dreams, the visions, and the words, but let's face it—the evidence of those promises being fulfilled is what keeps us going. We need that evidence. So what does evidence look like when you have yet to see? Honestly, we put too much of an emphasis on having evidence. I will gladly admit that we can be encouraged and strengthened by the evidence, but we can't measure our faith by evidence alone. Again, this is why it's so important to connect trust with our faith. When trust is constant, we don't need evidence to mandate our faith, but we will gladly receive the evidence so that we can be encouraged. But let's not overthink ourselves into a corner here. Ultimately the evidence is our faith.

Although there may be times when you feel limited, faith in the prophetic words over your life doesn't always require a blind faith. That's why you were given those dreams, those visions, and/or those words over your life. Faith is the evidence that you need! Look at it from the understanding of what Paul wrote to the Ephesians when he told them that they were dead in their trespasses and sins. A life that they no longer walked in according to the standard of the world. Paul acknowledged that the prince of the power of the air was working in those who chose disobedience. Those who were in Christ once knew the lusts of the flesh along with the desires of flesh and mind. As Paul reminded the church, because of God we are rich in mercy. God's love is great, and even during the time we were dead in our transgressions we were made alive together in Christ. Paul encouraged you and me with the reality that we are raised with Christ and seated with Him in heavenly places. We are spiritually strengthened in the realization that it was by grace we were saved through faith. It wasn't something that you or I could do for ourselves so that we could one day boast about what we had accomplished. We are created in Christ for good works, which God Himself prepared so that we would walk in them.

THE EVIDENCE

Your faith in Christ is the evidence of who you are because of Him. There's your evidence! When you know who He is, you know who you are. Your faith is the evidence that you've been looking for. You're trying to build yourself through the lens faith so that you can see the fulfillment of your prophetic promises and it has been there the whole time. Although you want to have faith in yourself, or in humankind, man (including yourself) will fail you. It's why we find ourselves frustrated. We have the tendency to misappropriate our faith.

The Bible never tries to prove that God exists through evidence. If that was the case there would be no need for faith in Him. Think about how the Bible starts: *"In the beginning God"* (Gen. 1:1). That's not a whole lot of evidence, but consider what Psalms 14:1 says, *"The fool has said in his heart, 'There is no God.' They are corrupt, they have committed abominable deeds; there is no one who does good."*

In his letter to the Romans, Paul took into consideration what they would encounter as the Gospel spread through the whole world. Paul sincerely cared for the Romans, and when we read his letters we too can find encouragement in his words. We are reminded of his willingness to preach the Gospel without any shame because the heart of the Father was for everyone to believe and be saved. We know that the righteous man is called to live by faith, but this is often the most difficult in the midst of our trials. Yet Paul reminds us that God is clearly against ungodliness and unrighteousness. The wickedness of humankind has the tendency to smother truth and keep people from acknowledging the truth about God.

In reality, God has placed within us the knowledge that there is a God. We cannot excuse those who oppose the truth on the claim of ignorance. When we look at the creation of the world, God has a way of making what is invisible now visible. Ultimately this leaves everyone without an excuse; they know there is a Creator. When we take the time to study the scriptures, we see the fingerprints of God on humankind. Sadly, throughout history humankind has often refused to honor Him as Lord and, at times, also refused to be thankful for His loving-kindness. In times of trial and testing we have often entertained foolish thoughts that led us into darkness. When our faith is being challenged, we replace faith with logic and soon become beings of super intelligence, only to reveal we are often fools.

This is a warning to us as sons and daughters of God. We must stay devoted to the Lord, lest He remove His hand from us and turn us over to a reprobate mind. I honestly don't know how an individual could ever go that far, but I do know that when Paul wrote the Romans he stressed the importance of not giving in to moral depravity. Don't trade the truth of God for a lie! I am not trying to scare anyone, but I am doing my best to get you to understand the importance of our relationship with the Lord. We are in the midst of a lustful generation in which men and women have ignored the natural order and exchanged normal sexual relations for homosexuality. The current generation considers it to be worthless to accept the true knowledge of God. Sadly, we are witnessing every kind of evil, greed, and cruelty. People are filled with jealously, conflict, and strife. Everywhere you look these days there are hateful disagreements and arguments. Many are liars and full of gossip, who love to spread malicious slander.

We haven't even talked about the egos of those who are nothing more than arrogant boasters. In our day it seems that people no longer honor their parents; they are ruthless, heartless, and without mercy. It's very sad to see because we know that they are aware of God yet they still choose to go into darkness and encourage others to do the same, cheering them on when they do.

We actually have more evidence that proves we shouldn't deny the existence of God rather than evidence that God exists. The evidence is not about proving whether or not God is who He says He is. We are so desperate at times for the evidence that marks our prophetic promises that we fail to remember who He is. We put way too much emphasis on humankind and ourselves. The moment that we feel like the evidence isn't strong enough for us, we find ourselves bailing on those prophetic promises. When the Lord gives us a prophetic vision of our loved one serving Him but they continue to dive deeper and deeper into sin, that lack of evidence determines our level of faith in the not yet seen.

It becomes dangerous when we focus on evidence more than faith. When evidence is presented in court, it is done to prove a point true or false. When we demand evidence for the prophetic promises God gave us, we are putting God on trial to determine whether He is faithful or guilty of failing to come through. The *evidence of things not yet seen* is for our faith in the Word of the Lord and the reality of who God is.

THE BLUEPRINT OF FAITH

So what is the blueprint of faith? Every blueprint is individually stamped. My blueprint may not look like your blueprint. It's why we can't get caught up in comparison. Our blueprints will have similarities, but they will not be identical in nature. Why? Because your prophetic dreams, your prophetic visions, or your prophetic words may not be what mine are. There will be promises in which we overlap because of our kingdom assignments, but for the majority of us the blueprint of faith will be our own design.

You are the architect of your faith. God is the master builder, but you determine how and what you will do with your faith. The Lord will not force faith into your life. He will not force you to believe or deny. He will give you what is written in the Word for reminders and encouragement. He will give you a multitude of personal testimonies you can find encouragement through. God has given you the tools that you need to advance. You determine what you do with those tools. The problem is that when we have received these prophetic promises, we throw everything over to the Lord and sit back waiting for Him to do everything for us. That's why we can get so easily frustrated with God when we don't see our promises unfolding in our lifetime.

Think about the children of Israel and what they saw while in bondage.

They saw the Nile turn to blood.

Can you imagine that the major source of your life suddenly is no longer acceptable to you and your family due to this kind of transformation?

They saw frogs appear from nowhere.

How would you have responded to a massive multitude of frogs all around you? It's simple to talk about, but for one moment imagine the chaos that would be occurring.

They saw the abundance and increase of lice.

Every parent has gone through the scare of their kids coming home from school with lice. Some parents have had to endure the hardship of stripping down clothes and bedding, fumigating everything in the house, buying special shampoo and soap in desperate attempts to stop the lice. Now multiply that by 100 times.

They saw darkness cover the land.

I recognize that there are certain parts of the world that have no sunlight for many days or months. Because of a long history with that, they have learned to deal with the challenges. How would your day be affected if you never had this kind of environment and out of nowhere the sun disappeared?

They saw hail fall from the sky and burn at the same time.

There are a lot of things that we could list that seem impossible. I would quickly say that hail burning would be one of those things. My mind has a difficult time comprehending this, and yet it happened.

They saw disease kill cattle.

Everything you have is invested in your livestock. Sickness invades the camp and in a swift moment every single cow is gone from a disease you have never seen before.

They saw the firstborn die.

There are a lot of things humankind may be able to endure, but the loss of a child is at the top of the list as something no one should ever have to go through. When this happened in Egypt, it happened to many families and not just one.

They experienced the Red Sea divide and walked on dry land.

Perhaps this is one of the more astonishing aspects of the escape from Egypt. Standing before a river and seeing that river separate, creating a path to walk through, is amazing to say the least. But the crazy part is really in the fact that they walked across on *dry* land. Can you imagine their faces!

They experienced the cloud by day and fire by night.

Man has always had the ability to pioneer. Some of our childhood heroes were the men and women who dared to go where no one had been before. They would depend upon the stars, the land, and sometimes the patterns of the weather. Now imagine you're leaving Egypt and your guidance isn't the North Star or even the land. You have the Presence of the Lord manifested both day and night. Simply amazing!

They witnessed water from a rock.

If you have been to a stream or a creek you have witnessed water running over and around rocks. What would it have been like to stand there in need of water, in the midst of dry land, without hope, a parched throat, and you see water emerge from a rock? That alone should cause your faith to increase.

They witnessed manna on the ground for 40 years.

I think about this often. In the early days I would have been grateful, but I also consider that I may not be as thankful once I got burned out on manna. Yet there is something that really stands out here—they were provided for!

Despite everything that they saw or experienced personally, an entire generation had to be removed before they entered into the promised land. Though they saw God move in supernatural ways, the battle to fully trust in the Lord continued to hinder their faith. Only Joshua and Caleb would enter the land that was promised. The blueprint of faith is determined by what you are willing to embrace through hope, faith, and trust in the God who spoke to you in dreams, visions, and His Word.

> *"So then faith comes by hearing, and hearing by the word of God"* (Rom. 10:17). Notice it does not say, *faith comes from having heard.* The whole nature of faith implies a relationship with God that is current. The emphasis is on hearing...in the now!
> —BILL JOHNSON, *When Heaven Invades Earth: A Practical Guide to a Life of Miracles*

CHAPTER 7

THE JOURNEY

"Time moves so quickly, and no matter who we are or what we have done, the time will come when our lives will be over. As Jesus said, 'As long as it is day, we must do the work of him who sent me. Night is coming, when no one can work' (John 9:4). ...Life is short, and every day is a gift from God."
—BILLY GRAHAM, *Just As I Am*

In 2009, my wife and I took a position at a church as student pastors. It was the first time I entered the ministry as full-time staff at a church. I left my job in the textile industry behind, and with a huge leap of faith we left our families nine hours away as well. It was a very difficult move leaving our parents and siblings behind.

Very few understood why we were doing what we were doing. I was questioned multiple times about how I could remove our children from their grandparents and aunts and uncles. It seemed like no one understood the importance of being obedient to the call of the Lord. It was easy for others to play the devil's advocate and declare we were wrong while never considering the fact that God had called us to say yes. That yes involved our lives being uprooted from the place I had always known to be home.

We returned back home in 2013 for a brief period of time only to relocate to another town in the state and eventually another state seven hours away. Our lives became the existence of saying yes to the Lord no matter the trials that we had to endure. There were times that I missed it, and more times that those around us missed it. Those hardships taught us to withstand the storms of life. Those difficulties taught us to learn to put more and more faith in the Lord rather than trust in man. It's not that we can never trust man; it's more that our trust in God can never be compromised.

Remember the story from the preface to this book? It was the first Sunday of the year in the very back of my dad's church. The Lord whispered to me, *"You don't understand faith the way that I need you to know it."*

Honestly, that statement from the Lord did not please me. It actually frustrated me. I couldn't believe what I was hearing. *Faith* was one of those areas that I took a lot of pride in. Over the years of my walk with Christ, I strove to have a strong walk of faith. It was this mindset that drove me to take those huge steps in obedience. You might even say that my faith had become something that I was a bit arrogant about. I took pride in my faith, and now God was telling me that I understood nothing about faith. That's a difficult pill to swallow.

In over twenty-one years of being a follower of Christ and in ministry, I never once connected faith and the prophetic. Every example I had of faith was in the realm of saying yes to what God was saying to do or where to go. Although I had been involved with prophetic ministry for a number of years, it never once registered with me that prophetic dreams, visions, and words had to have faith applied to them. I know that sounds crazy. Many of you will read this and say, "How could you not connect the dots of faith and the prophetic?" There is a difference between believing in God and applying faith to fight for the fulfillment of our prophetic promises. Most people will have faith in what is given to us (whether through a dream, vision, and/ or word), but we fail to apply faith to see it through.

That same year, three months later, my mother called me in tears to report that the doctors had told her she had cancer. What I am about to say may sound a little crazy to some, but the very moment that my mother told me that she had cancer I immediately had a rush of faith come all over me. I instantly remembered a time many years prior. I remembered my mother calling me when I was about 25 years old and our oldest daughter was 4 years old and our youngest daughter was a baby. My mother had the same dream for many nights in a row. Although I was young in the Lord, I had already been a senior pastor and was then serving as an associate pastor. My mother called me seeking advice as to why she might be having the same dream every night. The dreams keep occurring for about two weeks. In my mother's dream, she was playing outside with her grandkids. She was a lot older than she was in real life at the time, and there were over a dozen grandchildren with her, but they weren't little kids. The grandkids were grown in the dream.

The very moment I heard my mother crying, I remembered her dream. I remembered that she was older and the grandkids were grown. What my mother didn't know was that the Lord had been preparing me for this call. When He spoke to me on that first Sunday in January, he had taken me on a very specific journey. For those three months, the Lord was teaching me about the prophetic and how to fight for the promises in dreams, visions, and/or prophetic words. The Lord had prepared me for this, and I realized that the cancer was an attempt from the enemy to prematurely take my mother from this world. The enemy had a plan, but the Lord gave me a strategy.

I had learned that many times in our lives the Lord will give us a dream, a vision, or a word in which we are a lot older than we may be when we receive that word. The Lord gives us those words as encouragement to get us to live our lives in hope and expectation. This happened in the life of Abraham when the Lord gave him a vision of Jesus on Moriah. Had Abraham not been given that vision, he may have never gone through with the sacrifice of Isaac. The Lord provided a ram, but not without the price of a test. You are going to be tested. Many times, those tests will be from the enemy, and other times they may be from the Lord. Yes, contrary to what we want to believe, the Lord will test you.

Because of the research that I had done concerning faith, trust, hope, Abraham, and the others mentioned in Hebrews 11, I was prepared for the phone call. When my mother told me she had cancer, I instantly knew that the cancer would not be her death certificate. It wasn't me trying to be strong for my mother. It was faith connecting to the prophetic promise of her life. I knew that the enemy was trying to prematurely take my mother from her destiny through cancer. But the enemy failed to realize that the Lord had prepared me.

I remember telling my mother on the phone, "Mom, it's okay to cry. You have been given news that has shaken you and God isn't mad because you're crying. Go ahead and cry, but know this—you will *live* and *not* die. Mom, listen to me, the Lord has already given me a word and it's because of that word that I know that you are going to get through this. Mom, you are going to *live*."

When the ministry trip was over, we came back home to be with my mother and dad as she was facing a double mastectomy. All of the family were there that day. The doctor came in to explain everything to my dad, me, and my siblings. While my mother was in surgery, I sat my dad and siblings down. I remember saying to them, "If you want to cry you can, but I want you all to know that I am not going to cry. I'm not going to let Mom see me cry. I have a word from the Lord and I need to be the demonstration of that word; therefore, it's important that I keep a picture of strength before her at all times." It was never my goal to be cocky or arrogant with my confidence; rather, it was my goal to remain strong. I knew that there would be days when the faith of my mother, dad, and siblings would be tested. I had to be strong for my family and myself.

The doctor came out and told the family that the surgery went well and they had removed all of the cancer. Yep, they removed the cancer. I heard it with my own ears and it would be something that I would remember. My mother had a decision to make concerning chemo and radiation. For the type of cancer that she was diagnosed with, her medical team strongly recommend that she receive chemo and radiation treatments.

At this point, some may second-guess me and the faith that I had concerning the life of my mother. Let me be clear that I never wavered one ounce to whether or not she would live. I knew the mentality that my mother would have throughout this whole process. I knew there would be days when her faith would be strong, but there would be days when her faith would be almost gone. I kept telling my dad that it's important that we keep mom mentally strong because the moment she gives up mentally we will never change her mind.

My mother is a phenomenal woman of God, but all of us have our weaknesses. My mother is the picture of a true southern belle. Standing five feet two inches with a petite frame and blond hair, my mother would often be mistaken for Dolly Parton. It was very funny at times, and of course I ran with it when I could. Mom grew up in an area where we often focus on the negative before we can see the positive. It came natural at times. For some people, it's very challenging to see the rainbow because of the clouds. But you never get to see the rainbow without the rain.

I remember sitting with my mother and she was very concerned over losing her hair. I had already done a lot of research and was shocked with the stories of how people had endured chemo and radiation and never lost their hair. Although people usually lose their hair, it does not happen every single time. I remember telling Mom, "Mom, do you believe that God can protect your hair from falling out?"

She looked at me. "Yes, I know He can...but you know that the doctor told me that I would lose my hair." I shook my head and asked again, only to get the same response. I asked a third time, and I got the same response again. I knew then that I wasn't going to get her to agree. So I began to work diligently reminding her and Dad about the word that I got.

CAN'T-CER

The days turned into weeks and eventually months. On a particular visit with my parents, we were in the living room and my dad said something as an encouragement to my mother. Instantly my mother snapped, screamed at my dad, and went into the bedroom. My mother was falling apart physically, mentally, and spiritually. The journey had become more than she could endure. From the bedroom I heard my mother call my name. I stood up and took a deep breath. Up to this time, I had not shed a single tear over my mother's illness. Actually, I had renamed cancer to "can't-cer." I was my mother's oldest son and I took my birthright as her oldest and I told can't-cer every day that it couldn't have my mother. I never said it could (hence the "can" in *cancer*).

As I stepped into her bedroom she was sitting on the edge of the bed. I looked at a frail five-foot-two woman who was weakened by the effects of chemo and radiation. She was wearing a cap to cover her bald head. I hadn't seen my mother without hair. Months had passed but I had never seen her bald. I didn't know if I could handle seeing her without hair. As I walked to her I kept telling myself, "Don't cry now. Don't let her see you cry. She can't see you cry." She reached up, pulled the cap off of her head and asked me to come closer. That frail little southern belle lay her head on my chest and told me what I did not want to hear. She said, "Ryan, I can't do this anymore. I can't keep going through what I am going through. I want to quit. Ryan, I am ready to die. I just want to go ahead and die."

It had come to this moment, and I had to do the unthinkable. I placed my hands on my mother's shoulders and pushed her off of my chest. I proceeded to say, "Mom, I need you to look at me as a man of God. I need you for one moment to look at me as God's son and not your son. I need you to listen to me as a man of God and not your little boy." Something rose up within me and I began to talk to my mother in a manner that I never imagined talking to her. It was with a voice of authority and it was directed to shake her out of where she was. "Mom, listen. You will *live* and you will *not* die. I have a word from the Lord. Mom, you are going to get through this. I am asking you to give me forty days to fast and pray for you and your mind. Mom, promise me that you won't do anything until the forty days have passed. I will fight for you because I know that you can't fight for yourself. Give me forty days, and after those days have passed, if you still want to die I will pray you into eternity. But for the next forty days, I will fight for you. Mom, I have a word!" She looked up at me with tears in her eyes and she agreed to give me those forty days.

We left that day with a new assignment for this journey. Forty passed in prayer and fasting. I knew that my mother was on the verge of mentally checking out. Both my dad and I recognized how important it was to keep her mentally strong. On day forty-one, my cell phone rang. It was my mother. "Ryan, I don't want to die. I want to live. I have a reason to live. I have grandbabies to see grow up and play with."

Yes! I knew that Mom was on the turnaround. I never once told her about the word that I had received. I never reminded her about the dreams she had so many years ago. I simply stood on the prophetic promises of her life. I know that somewhere during those forty days, the Lord reminded my mother of the dreams she had so many years prior. That's exactly what happened. My mother came out of those forty days with a different mindset. It was like she could see herself getting through everything for the first time. She was recognizing that she was going to live and not die. Although she still had weeks of radiation remaining on her time frame, she was different. She was going to live.

It was a fight, but it was from the place of a prophetic dream. When my mother originally had that dream night after night, she only had three grandchildren. During her journey through can't-cer, she had ten grandchildren with the oldest being very young teenagers. While I am writing this, my parents now have eleven grandchildren with the oldest being 21 and the youngest being a small infant. We are still a long way from the grandchildren being grown. It's why I was so strong in my faith of the prophetic promise that God had given to her through a dream. I knew that because the children were so young, this disease trying to destroy my mother was not from the Lord. By the way, my mother has been can't-cer-free for years now.

Now, when you read this Hebrews 11:13 and Hebrews 11:39-40 may cross your mind. Those heroes of faith never lived to see their promises fulfilled. There may come a day when my mother leaves this world and she never gets to play (in this world) with grown grandchildren, but I knew that it was way too early for her to be taken out. When I first received the call, I just instantly knew that it was not her time. Holy Spirit discernment told me that this was an attempt to prematurely end her life. I looked at the ages of my children and thought about the ages of my niece and nephews. It wasn't adding up. This was the enemy, but the Lord gave me a strategy. I had a key to the revelation of faith in our prophetic promises. This was an Abraham and Isaac moment. Like Abraham, we had to endure the test, but with the test came a glimpse from a distance that would get us beyond where we were.

THE FIGHT FOR FULFILLMENT

God had given my mother a prophetic dream; we just had to fight for the promise. God has given you a prophetic dream. God has given you a prophetic vision. God has given you a prophetic word. The question is, will you fight to see those words come to pass? We can't continue to put these words up on a hypothetical shelf where we fail to cultivate these words and see the promises activated by our faith. For many it isn't as challenging when we see those things come to pass, but what if our journey comes with only what can be seen from a distance? In other words, would you be okay with the Lord giving you a word and you never seeing it fulfilled in your lifetime?

For most of us we would prefer to see that word fulfilled in our lifetime. And yet, here is where we miss the point of our journey. Let me explain it this way: as mentioned in Chapter 5, over the years I have met men and women who have become bitter and angry toward God late in their lives. Why where they angry? They had prophetic promises involving their child bound in addiction. They were encouraged that their child would be set free, but over time their faith has been eroded while their anger has increased. How could someone endure the hardships that they have endured and not become bitter? God gave them hope. God gave them a glimpse. God gave them a promise. And now it appears that God lied.

This is why connecting our faith to prophetic promises is so vital. When God gives us those dreams, visions, and words, we have to recognize that it's His word.. Because it is His, it could never be something that it is not. The Lord cannot lie, nor would He give you false hope. It's not that God would show you something and then rip it out from underneath you. The problem is when we validate it based on whether or not we see it in our lifetime. You can't get into the habit of determining that your dreams, visions, and words are only accurate if you see them fulfilled during your life. Though we know this, sadly it happens every single day. It's overwhelming at times when you are striving to have the faith to see something revealed. I'm not saying that the journey is easy, but I am saying that it's worth the fight.

When I first met my wife, I was told stories about her grandfather, Robert, who was a man of God but passed away at a very young age. I never met the man, but some of the stories still have power to this day. One particular story is that of my father-in-law (my wife's step-dad). When my mother-in-law was dating her future husband, he did not have a relationship with Jesus as his Savior. My father-in-law came from a very religious background that had his mind caught in captivity. It was Robert telling his daughter, my mother-in-law, that it was okay for her to marry the man she was dating. Although he wasn't born again, Robert had a vision from the Lord showing him that my father-in-law would be born again and serve the Lord with his life. Not long afterward, Robert sat down in a chair and crossed over into eternity with a massive heart attack. He never lived to see his future son-in-law say yes to Jesus. And yet, he did see his future son-in-law say yes— he saw it from a distance. (By the way, many years later, my father-in-law did receive Christ as his Savior.)

Before I close this chapter out, I want to stress that I do not always understand why certain things unfold the way that they do. I know that some may be reading this and asking why their loved one died. Honestly, I don't know. There are a million reasons that I don't think, see, nor understand as the Lord does. I realize that there are times we fight for those we love, and yet they step into eternity. I don't have the answer to why this happens.

This is what I do know—regardless of what you or someone you love is going through, there is a prophetic promise to fight for. There is a reason to fight and sometimes that fight is done with them, and sometimes it is done in place of them. We have to get to the place where we are okay with the possibility of not seeing it. We need to get to the place where we learn how to fight for the promises through faith, with trust, and by hope because we have seen them prophetically being fulfilled. We can't become angry at the Lord because the journey is too difficult. We need to learn how to fight for the promises. Whether we see them now or from the distance, we know that God is not a liar. Therefore, when He gives you that dream, that vision, or that word, you have a reason to fight for the fulfillment of the prophetic promises. The journey may be filled with ups and downs, but your journey is marked by the promises of the Lord!

I know that there will be a day when my mother steps into eternity. But until that day comes, I will fight and help my mom fight for the fulfillment of the prophetic promises. I will contend!

CHAPTER 8

THE ACTIVATION OF FAITH

"The truth is, trials will come. The truth is, warfare will come. The truth is, temptations will come—and positive thinking and positive confessions will not stop them from coming. But here is the truth you should focus on: God loves you, and your faith pleases Him."
—JENNIFER LECLAIRE,
The Making of a Prophet

"Then he said to me, 'This is the word of the Lord to Zerubbabel saying, "Not by might nor by power, but by My Spirit," says the Lord of hosts"'
—ZECHARIAH 4:6

The activation of your faith depends upon you, but you must also recognize that it's not by your power or strength. We have to remember that every man is given a measure of faith (see Rom. 12:3), but that faith isn't limited because the Lord has provided the increase. I am convinced that the measure of faith that we have been given is not always going to be enough. When you get the phone call from the doctor and they say you have cancer, it won't always be enough. When your child is bound by crystal meth, that measure won't always be enough. When your marriage is failing and quickly falling apart, it won't feel like it is enough. Why would the Lord only give us a measure knowing that we would need more?

> *For to one is given the word of wisdom through the Spirit, to another the word of knowledge through the same Spirit, to another faith by the same Spirit, to another gifts of healings by the same Spirit, to another the working of miracles, to another prophecy, to another discerning of spirits, to another different kinds of tongues, to another the interpretation of tongues. But one and the same Spirit works all these things, distributing to each one individually as He wills* (1 Corinthians 12:8-11 NKJV).

So many times when we discuss the gifts of Holy Spirit, we have the tendency to concentrate on the gift of tongues and the gift of prophecy. We like to focus on those two because we can see the manifestations quickly in our lives. Their activation can easily be spotted in a service. We will even embrace the gift of healing and miracles when the Lord moves mightily during a service and people are seeing legs straighten out or people getting out of wheelchairs. However, there is one of the nine gifts that we rarely ever hear anything about, and that is the gift of faith. Yep, although there are nine gifts mentioned here in First Corinthians 12, we rarely ever hear any sermons or teachings on this particular gift. The gift of faith is difficult to see in the natural; therefore, it's one of those gifts that gets moved to the back and forgotten at times.

Because it's one of the nine gifts, we have to be open to understanding why the Lord would give it. There is actually a gift specifically for faith. When you need faith the most, Holy Spirit can activate a supernatural faith in your life. This is so important to recognize because our faith can often be limited. You know those times when we tell ourselves that it's okay to have a little bit of unbelief (God understands, wink wink). In those times, the Lord is reminding you and me that He has given us the gifts of Holy Spirit for such a time as this. It's the baptism of faith that brings supernatural increase. When we can't go another day or continue in the midst of life, the Lord can bring the increase through the gift of faith. It's okay to realize that we need the increase. We are human, and we will definitely have those moments when our measure of faith won't always be enough. However, the Lord has given you and me the gift of faith for those times.

The activation of our faith is hidden with our ability to tap into the fullness of Holy Spirit. I know that some reading this will quickly say that they were baptized in Holy Spirit years ago, and it seems that their faith is weak or low. Although you were baptized in Holy Spirit years ago and you had an outward evidence of tongues during that time, we all have times when we need a refilling. That's not implying that we can lose what we gained through the baptism of Holy Spirit. I am simply saying that we all need a re-filling from time to time. It's okay to ask the Lord to give you a fresh baptism of faith. I want to encourage you, before the day ends, to ask the Lord to refill you again. You don't have to wait for a special service or guest speaker to lay hands on you. Right now, where you are, you can ask the Lord to baptize you again. Ask the Lord specifically to activate the increase of faith in your life. Ask the Lord and He will release a fresh baptism today!

Luke 8 and Mark 5 tell an encouraging story of activated faith. Jairus came pleading with Jesus to have Him come to his home to heal his daughter who was dying. In the midst of the journey there, a woman interrupted them due to the sickness that she had endured for twelve years. Imagine how Jairus felt the moment he saw Jesus stop and give His attention to the woman. It's important to remind ourselves that the reason Jesus stopped was because of what this woman did. When Jairus asked Jesus to come to the rescue of his daughter, Jesus never said a word to him; He simply began walking in the direction of their home. Now, Jairus was watching the time slip away as Jesus stopped to ask who touched Him. When the woman emerged, she was already healed from the moment that she touched the hem of His garment and the power left the body of Jesus, moving into the woman. Jesus spoke to her and told her that it was her *faith* that made her whole. For one moment, imagine you are Jairus. Jesus hasn't said anything to you and now He has stopped to have a conversation with an older woman. Your daughter is dying at home, but Jesus is dealing with the faith of this woman. You might have been frustrated, to say the least.

Then came the news—the daughter had died. Too much time had passed. *Now* Jesus addressed Jairus and told him that his daughter was not dead, only sleeping. The challenge before Jairus was whether or not he could trust what Jesus had declared. At this point, his faith had to have gone to nearly nothing. The report that his daughter was dead did nothing to increase his faith. However, because he did have faith in Jesus to heal his daughter, he would now have to trust Him when He said that his daughter wasn't dead, only sleeping.

Jesus did speak to Jairus, and He simply said not to fear but believe. The one time He spoke He spoke clearly about his faith. Though possibly in despair or weak in faith, the moment that Jesus walked into the room everything changed. Faith was activated because Jesus told Jairus to not have fear but to believe. When you have Jesus, all things are possible!

You and I don't have to live with the impossibilities that we face. We don't have to be overwhelmed by fear or beaten down by anxiety. Even if depression does its best to creep in or offense wants to root itself within our minds, we can have the faith to overcome in order to fight for our prophetic promises. Through the blood of Jesus, we have been reconciled and redeemed. The delay is not denial. Just because there is a delay on your journey it does not mean that God is denying you what He has already promised you.

Your prophetic promises are never hopeless with Jesus!

TESTED FAITH REVEALS VALUE WITHIN YOU

You have a living hope in the resurrection of Jesus through which you can obtain an inheritance that is imperishable and undefiled. Do you realize that it will never fade away? There is a reservation in heaven for you that is personally protected by the Lord. Your salvation is ready to be revealed through faith. You and I have a reason to rejoice, even if it's for a little while. When the trials come, they will prove your faith, which is more precious than gold. Do you understand that even gold is perishable when tested by fire? Faith is more precious when found in praise and in honor of Jesus Christ. Though you may have not seen Him, you have a sincere love for Him as you believe in Christ. Recognizing the value of your faith will cause you to rejoice.

REGARDLESS OF THE TRIAL, REMAIN FIRM

One of the more difficult aspects of life is standing strong in our faith when everyone else around us is reminding us of the potential outcomes. People are never the enemy, yet they are often the problem. We are commanded to love one another as Christ loved us. This can be rather challenging when people push us to our limits. It is why we must stand firm in our faith and remind ourselves that there is no greater love than one who lays down their life for their friends. We have a responsibility to be faithful unto the Lord no matter the trial. We have to know deep within ourselves that He chose us and appointed us so that we would go forth and bear the fruit of the Father.

Jesus said that whatever we ask of the Father in His name He will give to you.

THE REWARD IS WORTH EVERY TRIAL

Whenever the days get difficult for me personally, I remind myself of Joseph and all that he had to endure. He never knew why these things were happening to him, and every time it appeared his hope would be fulfilled, he was set back another step. When I read the story of Joseph, there are no scriptures that talk about him despairing or being willing to give up. What we do see as a theme in his life is that Joseph was constant in his faith.

With that in mind, let's be willing to trust in the Lord fully. Let us embrace God's correction in our lives so that we grow and mature because we know that a loving Father does this for His children. That's a trial few of us want to talk about. No one likes correction, but correction is necessary for growth. We should be willing to welcome God's discipline because it also validates authentic sonship. We must learn that if we have never once endured correction, it only proves we are not sons. That's a difficult test, but a test that must be proven. Discipline seems to be more pain than pleasure at the time, but it will produce a transformation of your character, righteousness, and peace.

COUNT IT ALL JOY

Consider it all joy, my brethren, when you encounter various trials, knowing that the testing of your faith produces endurance. And let endurance have its perfect result, so that you may be perfect and complete, lacking in nothing (James 1:2-4).

I cannot help but to laugh every time I come across this scripture as I am reminded of a conversation I had many years ago as a young pastor of a small rural church in Alabama. I preached a message on counting it all joy, and after the message I remember my mother asking me if I was implying that every time she went to the mailbox and got a bill she was to count it all joy that she received a bill. I can actually still see my mother acting this out as she waved her hands in the air, overemphasizing her joy. This is not exactly how James would describe counting it all joy. James is challenging you and me to recognize the joy in the midst of our trials. What joy? How can there ever be joy in a trial? James tells us that we find our joy in knowing that the test of our faith will produce endurance, and with that we will lack nothing. It seems ridiculous at first, but we can actually have joy in the test because our faith reminds us that we will endure without lack!

YOUR WORDS MATTER

The truth is, I could write another book on the importance of the words we speak, and the words that we listen to. One of the greatest lessons that our family learned through my mother's journey with can't-cer was to guard what we spoke into my mother's life. During the early days of mom's diagnoses, many people wanted to visit my parents' house and share their own stories of going through cancer. I remember calling my parents and begging them to let me speak to certain individuals who kept speaking into their lives. Some people had the best of intentions but just didn't recognize the damage they were causing with their words.

In those early days many would share horror stories, bad reports, bad doctor experiences, and more. They would tell my mother what to expect and how bad it was going to be. I would call home and remind my mother that just because another woman had gone through breast cancer, it did not mean that she would endure the same things that they did. We, as humankind, have this strange obsession with sharing our own experiences. In retelling those events, we think everyone else is going to suffer the same way that we did. Over a period of time, the stories began to impact my mother and my father. Fear crept into their thoughts, and before long their vocabulary began to change. The words that others had spoken into their life inadvertently affected the words coming out of their own mouths.

I cannot reiterate this enough. You have to guard your ear gates so that your heart cannot become contaminated and, before you realize the damage, you begin speaking death rather than life. Not long ago I sat down with my parents and asked them if they would do anything different if they were to live that journey over again. Without hesitation, my mother said that she wouldn't allow people to speak into her life with their horror stories again. People may mean well, but you have to be very cautious with the words you dwell upon. It's ultimately why I still refuse to say "cancer" and call it can't-cer—because I never said it could.

> *Death and life are in the power of the tongue, and those who love it will eat its fruit* (Proverbs 18:21).

YOUR PROMISES ARE MARKED BY WHO DWELLS IN YOU

You have to know that you are always loved by God! You may not fully comprehend it, but you have been positioned to be holy. God is equipping you with mercy and compassion for one another. The challenge before us all is to remain humble and not become someone who is easily offended. Because you know the Lord is for you,

you don't see the weaknesses in others as an opportunity to be better than them. Rather, you recognize the opportunity to demonstrate the goodness of the Father. Even in moments of finding fault with someone, it is your responsibility to forgive as you have been forgiven. The promises for your life are not solely for you and no one else. You must understand that those promises will also impact your family, your friends, and those you may never meet. They will see the work of the Lord and know that if He is for you then He is also for them.

You are marked by the love of the Father, and you demonstrate that love as your heart guides you with a peace that cannot be fully described, only experienced. In this life, you and I must remain thankful in bad times and good times. Choose to be thankful. Allow the Word of Christ to live in you. Don't just read the words on the pages as if the Bible is just another book; allow those words to challenge you daily and help you to instruct others who may not be where you are. Never, ever, fail to remember what God has done for you!

I share this to remind you and encourage you that you have more than enough reason to activate the faith that is within you. Granted, there are times we are weak, but that's why the Word of the Lord is so valuable to you and me. We need to remind ourselves so that we can be encouraged daily. We can't end up like those who only believe for a while. We can't have our prophetic promises fall to the ground without being cultivated with our faith, hope, and trust in the Lord. It's so easy to believe today, but will you still be standing strong ten years from now? Will you be as convinced forty years down the road of your prophetic promises as you were the moment that you first had the dream, the vision, or the word?

In Luke 8, we find a passage of scripture where these huge crowds gathered together from many towns to hear Jesus tell parables. In one particular parable, Jesus shared about a farmer who went to sow seed in his fields for a harvest. This particular farmer scattered his seed in different soil. Some of that seed fell on a pathway that was very hard-packed. Because of that, the seed wasn't able to grow and became good only for the birds. The farmer scattered some of his seed on gravel, but because of that it couldn't take root and ultimately could not gain the proper moisture it needed to grow. The farmer scatter some of his seed where there was nothing but weeds. Like the times before, the seed was unable to grow due to being choked out by the weeds. Finally, the farmer was able to scatter some of his seed into good, fertile soil. In that ground the seed grew and flourished, producing more than a hundredfold harvest for the farmer.

I know that when we read this story, we say that if this was us, we wouldn't make the same mistakes as the farmer. Isn't it interesting how we always know better if it was us and not them? Hindsight will teach us a lot.

Here is the truth of the matter. Jesus shared this parable to teach the disciples (and us) that there is so much more than what we may first perceive. Jesus was saying that we have been given a teachable heart to perceive the secret, hidden mysteries of God's kingdom. However, there are those who don't have a heart that is willing to listen. Because they aren't willing to listen, the Word of God is nothing more than stories to them. There are individuals who have eyes to see, but they are blind to the truth of God's Word. Though they listen, they are unable to receive full revelation.

We can never fail to understand that the Word of God is seed sown into our hearts. There are those who are like the hard path with hard hearts. They hear the Word of God but the slanderer quickly snatches away what is sown in their hearts. Because of this they are kept from believing Christ as their Savior and never truly experience salvation. Like the seed on the gravel, there are those who will respond to the Word with excitement, but when a difficult season from the enemy comes they fade away. They never took root in the truth; therefore, their faith is merely temporary. When seed falls into the weeds, those individuals hear the Word of God but their spiritual growth is choked off by their own cares, personal dreams, ambitions, and of course obtaining the riches of the world. Sadly, they place a higher value on the pleasures of life. They will never become mature and fruitful. Thankfully, there are those who are good ground. Ground that is fertile. These individuals love truth. They respond by clinging to every single word and encouraging themselves in faith. It is this seed that will one day bear a harvest!

There will always be those near you who will believe for a while, but in the passing of time the temptation to give up becomes too much for them. The truth is they had no firm root! You need to activate your faith and root it into your prophetic promises. Let those dreams, visions, and words become rooted by faith in what you see from a distance. Learn to keep the ground cultivated so that the weeds of time cannot kill the promises that the Lord revealed to you. If we see them in our lifetime, we rejoice. And if we do not live to see them, we rejoice because we have already seen them. We can't get to the place where our prophetic promises die because our hope was deferred.

> *Hope deferred makes the heart sick, but when the desire comes, it is a tree of life* (Proverbs 13:12 NKJV).

> *When hope's dream seems to drag on and on, the delay can be depressing. But when at last your*

dream comes true, life's sweetness will satisfy your soul (Proverbs 13:12 TPT).

Your faith begins to move, to act, when the power of God supernaturally empties you of doubt and fills you with a knowing. You come into a state of knowing that you know that you know. In that instant you cannot doubt.

—ORAL ROBERTS, *When You See the Invisible, You Can Do the Impossible*

CHAPTER 9

THE DESTINY OF YOUR FAITH

*"The opportunity of a lifetime needs to be
seized during the lifetime of the opportunity."*
—LEONARD RAVENHILL

By now you have possibly been stirred about your own dreams, visions, and words that have been spoken into your life. It's so important that you recall those words. You need to bring into remembrance what the Lord has spoken to you. You cannot afford to simply hear and/or see those words but never take the time to fight for the fullness. You can't get frustrated because it's not happening in the hour or the day you feel it should. You have to know that because God said it, that should be enough to settle it.

We have to bring to remembrance those words, not because the Lord fails to remember them Himself but so that we cultivate the promises.

REMINDING THE LORD OF HIS PROMISES

In Second Chronicles 20 we can read the story of Jehoshaphat. All of Judah was surrounded by three different enemies. At that time, it appeared that death was on the horizon for them. But Jehoshaphat knew the promises of the Lord. He knew what God had said, and he knew that those words had yet to be. I love how Second Chronicles 20:7 starts out: *"Are you not our God"* (NKJV). My goodness, what a powerful and bold declaration to the Lord from Jehoshaphat. It's important to see the confidence of Jehoshaphat—he knew the God whom he served. Many times in our trials, we begin to doubt whether or not God even said something. We are quick to doubt that God cares enough about us and our trials. We become weak in our faith and belief in who God declares that He is.

In this particular case, Jehoshaphat decreed a fast throughout the land and called for prayer to be established. While the fasting and praying were going on, the Lord began to speak to the prophet Jahaziel and give him instructions for Jehoshaphat and Judah. The prophet told Jehoshaphat to position the praise and worship leaders in the front and begin to play unto the Lord. As they began to worship the Lord, the scripture says that the three enemy camps that had surrounded Judah began to turn on one another and destroy every single person there. That literally means that the last two men standing killed one another, or the last man standing took his own life. The threat of the enemy was no more!

What would happened if we took the example of Jehoshaphat and applied it to our promises? In the midst of doubt, fear, and hesitation, we begin to fight for our promises instead of giving up because we feel like the enemy is greater than our promises. How many prophetic promises have stayed on shelves because we had more confidence in the abilities of our enemies than the power and authority of the Lord.

The passage of scripture also reminds us of how important it is to have the right kind of people surrounding you in your time of need. Everyone around you won't be the one you need. However, when you have the right people positioned to be there, you can have more victories than defeats. Jehoshaphat and Judah gathered together, they reminded the Lord of who He is and what He had said, and then the word of the Lord came, but it didn't come to Jehoshaphat. Rather, it came to the prophet, Jahaziel.

The first thing God said was, *"Do not be afraid"* (2 Chron. 20:15 NKJV). It reminds us of what Jesus said to Jairus when the report came in about his daughter. This is such a powerful scripture of encouragement as it reminds us that God will make a way when there seems to be no way. What would happen if we were a constant reminder of the promises of God? Would our trials cease to exist? No, trials will come and go. There will always be tests. Some of those tests will be from the Lord; not everything that challenges us is from the enemy. However, when we remind God about the promises that He spoke into our lives, and when we know who He is, it builds upon the foundation of our faith. It keeps us from having a double mind.

A FIRM FOUNDATION

When you are facing the most difficult times in your life, be encouraged—there is an opportunity to connect your faith in the Lord with the prophetic promises of your life and, in that, discover the joy of the Lord. When your faith is tested there will be power stirred up within you to help you endure and contend for your miracle. As your faith in the Lord grows stronger and stronger, you will discover that the Lord is working on you for His glory. The Lord is a good Father and He has the desire to give to you and me. Think about James 1:5: *"But if any of you lacks wisdom, let him ask of God, who gives to all gener-ously and without reproach, and it will be given to him."* We ask knowing that our faith in the Lord has no place for doubt. We have to be willing to be a person of strong faith and not someone who believes one minute and doubts the next.

When we are easily swayed in our faith we are like the ocean waves being tossed by the wind (see James 1:6). When we aren't contending through our faith, we find ourselves up one minute and down the next. Can you really expect to receive anything from the Lord when you're so easily tossed around as if you have no founda-tion in your life?

The destiny of your faith is in those dreams, visions, and words. Either your faith will lie dormant or you will consistently apply it to your prophetic promises. Contending for your prophetic promises will cause you to grow in faith, hope, trust, and mature spiritually. The tests that you will endure will build and strengthen you, not defeat you. The process and the time that passes might seem overwhelming at times, but your willingness to fight for those promises will strengthen you spiritually. When you are contending for your prophetic promises, you are doing it for the fulfillment over your life and for others who may be involved. Prophetic promises will always be more than just about you. There will always be others watching to see you fight for the promise. The test you are going through is so much bigger than you!

When you keep striking the ground (see 2 Kings 13:14-19), you learn to increase your faith over the prophetic promises of your life. You are contending for the promises over you, your family, your ministry, and/or your church. You could potentially also be fighting for the promises of your city, region, and/or state. Some of you could be fighting for this nation. It is so much more than just a dream, just a vision, or just a word. You need to learn to fight for the prophetic promises. Contend, strike the ground, fight, contend, strike the ground, fight—don't give in and don't give up!

The destiny of your faith is contingent upon your ability to contend for the prophetic. Contrary to what you may endure at the hands of humankind, you do have a real enemy called Satan. Satan and the demonic realm do not want you to succeed. They are satisfied with the defeat of those promises because they can recognize that you and your prophetic promises are a real threat to them. The moment that you are awakened to the reality that your dream, your vision, or your word has a destiny marked by fulfillment, it instantly becomes a threat to the enemy. I cannot stress it enough, but you have to learn to embrace the full armor of God. You can just read about it, but you must be willing to embrace every single piece in your life.

Finally, be strong in the Lord and in the strength of His might. Put on the full armor of God, so that you will be able to stand firm against the schemes of the devil. For our struggle is not against flesh and blood, but against the rulers, against the powers, against the world forces of this darkness, against the spiritual forces of wickedness in the heavenly places. Therefore, take up the full armor of God, so that you will be able to resist in the evil day, and having done everything, to stand firm. Stand firm therefore, having girded your loins with truth, and having put on the breastplate of righteousness, and having shod your feet with the preparation of the gospel of peace; in addition to all, taking up the shield of faith with which you will be able to extinguish all the flaming arrows of the evil one. And take the helmet of salvation, and the sword of the Spirit, which is the word of God. With all prayer and petition pray at all times in the Spirit, and with this in view, be on the alert with all perseverance and petition for all the saints, and pray on my behalf, that utterance may be given to me in the opening of my mouth, to make known with boldness the mystery of the gospel, for which I am an ambassador in chains; that

*in proclaiming it I may speak boldly, as I ought
to speak* (Ephesians 6:10-20).

In reality, you are not wrestling against your spouse,
your children, your boss or co-workers, your extended
family, etc., though it may appear that way. Your real
battle is against demonic powers that have waged war
against you and, more specifically, against your prophetic
promises. They know that God has a purpose and a destiny for you; therefore, they will do what they can to kill
the promises of your life. It is up to you to determine how
you will fight for those promises.

People are watching to see how you will contend for
the prophetic promises over your life. It may not always
feel like it, but you will be an encouragement to others
who are learning how to contend for the prophetic in
their own lives. The fulfillment of prophetic dreams,
visions, and words does not solely fall upon our shoulders. Again, this is why it is so important to know those
around you. Those individuals will either help to cata-
pult your faith or bring you down in defeat. You can't
have people around you who strive more in the realm of
common sense than those who walk with faith, hope,
and trust in the Lord. The voices of those around you
matter. Just ask Job.

*I have heard many such things; sorry comforters
are you all. Is there no limit to windy words? Or*

what plagues you that you answer? I too could speak like you, if I were in your place. I could compose words against you and shake my head at you. I could strengthen you with my mouth, and the solace of my lips could lessen your pain (Job 16:1-5).

The truth is that many people will give up. Churches will give up. Cities will forfeit their destiny. Sadly, they will give up. Sometimes they'll give up moments too soon. At the plateau of their breakthrough of promises fulfilled, they will quit. I can recall individuals, churches, ministries, and regions that have aborted promises prematurely as it became more than they were willing to fight for. Again, I am not implying that it's easy and we will never have weak moments in our journey. We all get weak, and there are times that we fall short. But, God! God who is strong in mercy, grace, and loving kindness will reignite the fire of our faith, causing us to contend.

You have been called to war in the Spirit: *"For I indeed, as absent in body but present in spirit, have already judged (as though I were present) him who has so done this deed"* (1 Cor. 5:3 NKJV). Our goal is to represent Christ in the fullness of who we are because of who He is. If the demonic realm knows the power and authority of Jesus, what do they do when we know who we are because of Christ in us? Jesus impacted entire cities and regions with transformation. When we study the life of Paul, we see that he also fought for prophetic promises everywhere he went as he fought from the revelation of who he was in Christ.

So, where do you go from here? Take the time to write down your prophetic promises. Write down that dream, that vision, and/or that word. Maybe you have multiple words that you are contending for. Write them down here. Begin to cultivate those words again. Keep going back and fighting for the fulfillment. Discover your joy in the Lord and know that what He said, He will deliver.

> Only believe, only believe. All things are possible, only believe.
> —SMITH WIGGLESWORTH, *The Complete Story*

CHAPTER 10

NOW FAITH IS

"Likewise today, some Christians are content to merely exist until they die. They don't want to risk anything, to believe God, to grow or mature. They refuse to believe his Word, and have become hardened in their unbelief. Now they're living just to die."
—DAVID WILKERSON

"And my message and my preaching were not in persuasive words of wisdom, but in demonstration of the Spirit and of power, so that your faith would not rest on the wisdom of men, but on the power of God."
—1 CORINTHIANS 2:4-5

NOW FAITH

How powerful are the words of Paul as he reminds us to depend on the Spirit of the Lord, and because of the Lord we can accomplish so much in the natural and spirit realm. Paul didn't address the Corinthians as an expert on the Word of the Lord, which should encourage us as well. He refused to impress others with some kind of eloquent speech or with deep words of wisdom. I am encouraged by the fact that Paul would admit to us that he felt inadequate at times. Paul understood the importance of the words he spoke and the message he shared. Unlike many preachers today, Paul wasn't trying to sway people with a persuasive argument because he knew that our faith had to be established through trust in the Lord and not in man's wisdom.

This is so important to know because there are things that have yet to be discovered or heard of before. There are things beyond our ability to imagine or comprehend, and these are the many things God has for those who love Him. There are things that God unveils prophetically that become reality to us by the Spirit. We have been given the opportunity to join together faith and the prophetic to see the revelations of God. In the natural, we are unable to understand any revelation without faith in the Lord. Holy Spirit helps to illuminate what was once hidden to us.

I believe that the real kicker is found in First Corinthians 2:9: *"Things which eye has not seen and ear has not heard, and which have not entered the heart of man, all that God has prepared for those who love Him."* There is so much more that the Lord wants to do for you and through you. Your life is not about enduring hardships until you make it heaven. It's more than just making it through the difficulties of life. You are called and destined to contend for the prophetic. Let me say it this way—faith is what's worth fighting for. If your level of faith is just enough to be born again and hope to make it to heaven, then your faith will just be that. However, when you know that the Lord has given you a dream, vision, or word, your faith is now more than just a hope. It's something that you are activating in order to see the fulfillment of your destiny.

It's time for you to rise up and stop holding on to that old-time religion. You need to have a "now" faith to ignite your prophetic promises. Rise up and leave the past behind you. Press toward the mark for the prize of the high calling of God in Christ Jesus (see Phil. 3:14). Apply a faith that's rooted and grounded in Jesus Christ. A faith that is grounded in the Word of God. If you fail to cultivate your faith with your prophetic promises, you see the increase of troubles in environment. Those promises did not come into your life to remain on a shelf and one day die. They came because of who God created and purposed you to be. Faith activated with your prophetic promises will move you beyond the typical old ways of thinking, eventually maturing you spiritually to a place where you do not waver with an unstable mind. Now faith connected to the prophetic allows us to believe and know that God is able to do what He says, when He declares it, and He goes about marking it to be fulfilled.

You need to leave behind what happened yesterday, no matter how many times you feel like you failed or others failed you—including the feeling that God may have failed you. When Satan wants to remind you of your past failures and mistakes, remind him of the prophetic promises declared over your life. When others try to disqualify you or attempt to discredit the truths of God's promises, remind them of the times that He moved and made a way that others deemed impossible. When you are at loss for a way out of the torment, the difficulties, and the hardships, keep striking the ground with your faith in the promises of the Lord. Know who God is and know who you are because of Christ in you.

PAUL AND TIMOTHY

Leonard Ravenhill, the evangelist, spent a majority of his life seeking after a revival that would forever alter a generation. He was devoted to a lifestyle of prayer and sought to cultivate the ground for a Holy Spirit breakthrough in revival. Late in Ravenhill's life a young man by the name of Steve Hill (an evangelist as well) relocated to Texas with the intention of being close to Ravenhill. Steve called Ravenhill one day and told him he wanted to meet Ravenhill, the man he had grown to admire so much. When the meeting was scheduled, Steve arrived at the door and knocked nervously on the lion brass door knocker. Leonard opened the door and shrugged his shoulders to Steve as if he was telling Steve that he was disappointed. He handed Steve a piece of paper, then he slammed the door shut. There Steve was standing at the closed door, wondering what had just happened. Steve opened the paper. It had words written on that paper that stated, "A man who is intimate with God is not intimidated by man." What? Why had Ravenhill handed this to Steve? He was teaching Steve a very valuable lesson. He was teaching Steve that if they were going to cultivate a relationship, Steve could not be intimidated by Leonard. Steve never moved. He just stood there at the closed door, and after a few minutes Leonard opened the door and said, "Well, come on in, young man."

Steve sat in Leonard's study describing how he had the desire to serve Leonard and be around him in any way that he could. What neither Steve nor Leonard knew was the Leonard's wife was listening to the conversation from the other room. When Steve left that day, Leonard's wife looked at him and said, "That's him; that's your

Timothy." From that moment Steve would serve the Ravenhills by cutting their grass, raking the leaves, and doing handyman work around the homestead there in Texas.

While Steve worked to help maintain their home, the relationship that Steve had with Ravenhill would often be nothing more than a 10- to 15-minute conversation in passing. I wonder how many of us would be that dedicated in serving someone. Over time, their relationship became stronger. Eventually it became clear that Steve indeed was like a Timothy to Leonard.

Leonard Ravenhill had a heart for revival. A revival that would see the nation affected by the outpouring. Years before that meeting with Steve, the Lord gave Leonard a prophetic promise that he (Leonard) would see the revival that would make the kind of impact that Leonard sought after. Leonard cultivated that word for years, and as each year passed he kept contending for the prophetic promise from the Lord. Then came the day that Leonard crossed over into eternity—November 27, 1994. So, did the prophetic promise of revival die when Leonard passed away? *No!*

Something significant was about to be launched, and Steve Hill would have a pivotal place in what God was doing. On Father's Day, June 18, 1995, a revival was birthed in Pensacola, Florida at Brownsville Assembly of God. Steve Hill was the guest speaker that day, and with the breath of God moving, they carried the mantle of revival for over four years, with over 200,000 people giving their life to Jesus. From the salvations to the baptisms in water and in Holy Spirit, the healings, miracles, and power of God were evident. Revival was birthed and Leonard got to see that manifested through his "Timothy," Steve Hill. The prophetic promise did not happen in Leonard's lifetime, but he was able to see the fulfillment of the promise through a spiritual son named Steve Hill. The prophetic promise in Leonard's life was worth fighting for.

Can you imagine what we have failed to see because we stopped contending for the prophetic? How many lives have been affected in a negative manner because someone stopped fighting for the fulfillment of those dreams, visions, and words? What have you given up on? Even more, by giving up without recognizing it, have you caused others to never see the glory of the Lord? It's never just about you as an individual. It's always about those nearest to us and those we may never know.

PROTECT YOUR PROMISE

In Matthew 25 there is the parable of the ten virgins. I know that when we read this parable our minds quickly go to end-time events. But I want us to read this and do our best not to think only on the end times but to look closely at the five foolish virgins. The biggest problem that the foolish ones had was that they were unwilling to do what they knew to do. It's not that the foolish ones had no idea how to fill their lamps or how to go about getting their oil. When you read the scripture you actually see that they knew exactly where to go to get their oil. That was never an issue. The problem was that they didn't want to pay the price for more oil. They wanted to rob those who had already paid the price. It was easier for them to rob those who had done what they weren't willing to do for themselves.

So many are like the five foolish virgins when it comes to the prophetic. Many individuals would rather live off of the faith of others. They rob from their faith, their hope, and their trust. Why? It's simple. They aren't willing to pay the price of faith, hope, and trust in the prophetic. If they can rob from others, they can live without having to contend or pay their own price. When they rob from others, it also means those others might miss their own fulfillments. When we live off of others, we will need them to fail along with us. We need those around us to have stories of failure so that we feel better about our own failures. Those who are unwilling to pay the price become satisfied in the missed opportunities of those around them. When you aren't willing to contend for the prophetic promises of your life, you will turn your attention on the destruction of prophetic promises in the lives around you.

> *The fear of the Lord is the beginning of wisdom, and the knowledge of the Holy One is understanding. For by me your days will be multiplied, and years of life will be added to you. If you are wise, you are wise for yourself, and if you scoff, you will bear it alone* (Proverbs 9:10-12 NKJV).

To those reading this book, I implore you to never forget that you only have one life to live. One opportunity of a lifetime to impact and potentially influence the world around you. The "fear of the Lord" should motivate you to make wise decisions that will impact your life and the lives of others.

Dreams, visions, and words are prophetic promises that know no boundaries of time. Now faith is not pretending. Faith can be in the prophetic promises. Now faith is not hoping that it's there. Faith is in knowing that the prophetic promise is there. Now faith is knowing because it has the substance, therefore faith is the substance that makes your prophetic promises before you. You must know that it exists within you and because you know it exists, your prophetic promises are there!

Sometimes you're going to be given a *third day* kind of faith. The reason I call it that is because of what

Abraham saw on the third day in Genesis 22:4. If we remember, Abraham saw the place from a distance on the third day. We have to ask ourselves again—what could he have seen on the third day in the land of Moriah?

What was the faith of Mary Magdalene like on the third day when she went to the tomb and discovered the body of Christ was gone? You see, we all need to experience a "third day" kind of faith and see our promise from a distance. I know that on the first day it seems like all of our hope is gone as the promises have been buried. When the second day comes around it seems as though there will never be any hope restored to us ever again. But on that third day when no one is expecting a resurrection of promise, we discover that there is a faith that can be connected to a prophetic promise and death cannot hold that promise down. You see, when you activate that "third day" faith to your prophetic promises, you will see the fulfillment of the Lord. Whether in this life or from a distance, you will welcome the promises.

I want to encourage you right now to take this time and ask the Lord to baptize you with the gift of faith. Some of you reading this may be saying that you have already been baptized in Holy Spirit. That is awesome, but I want to encourage you to specifically call upon the Lord to reignite the gift of faith in your life. Begin to call to the Lord and ask Him to fill you again. Ask the Lord to come now and fill you with His Spirit. The Lord wants more for you and is freely giving to you and me. Before you close the pages of this book, I prophesy to you that the Lord will increase the gift of faith in your life. You will see the prophetic promises of the Lord. You will lay hands on the sick and they will be made whole. You will have enough faith for those who may be weak in their trials. You will see the glory of the Lord!

About Ryan Johnson

Ryan is dedicated to helping equip the Body of Christ to awaken the nations with a prophetic call of a rising Ekklesia. He is a son of God, husband, and father of four. Ryan is a prophetic voice devoted to the righteousness of Christ, with the demonstration of the Father's Heart in regions, individuals, and the Church across the world.

On November 30, 1997, Ryan gave his life to Christ and immediately began serving the Lord. Ryan has served as a senior pastor, associate pastor and students pastor. Ryan is now a full-time itinerant minister traveling throughout the United States and many different nations. Ryan and his family now reside in Panama City, Florida, where he also serves as an overseer for High Praise Leadership School of Ministry with High Praise Worship Center.

For more information about Ryan, please visit:
www.ryanjohnson.us